P9-DFL-341

SO, WHAT DO YOU DO?

SO, WHAT DO YOU DO?

Discovering the
GENIUS *Next Door*
with One Simple Question

JOEL COMM

New York

SO, WHAT DO YOU DO?
Discovering the GENIUS *Next Door with One Simple Question*

© 2014 Joel Comm. All rights reserved.

No part of this publication may be reproduced or transmitted in any form or by any means, mechanical or electronic, including photocopying and recording, or by any information storage and retrieval system, without permission in writing from author or publisher (except by a reviewer, who may quote brief passages and/or show brief video clips in a review).

Disclaimer: The Publisher and the Author make no representations or warranties with respect to the accuracy or completeness of the contents of this work and specifically disclaim all warranties, including without limitation warranties of fitness for a particular purpose. No warranty may be created or extended by sales or promotional materials. The advice and strategies contained herein may not be suitable for every situation. This work is sold with the understanding that the Publisher is not engaged in rendering legal, accounting, or other professional services. If professional assistance is required, the services of a competent professional person should be sought. Neither the Publisher nor the Author shall be liable for damages arising herefrom. The fact that an organization or website is referred to in this work as a citation and/or a potential source of further information does not mean that the Author or the Publisher endorses the information the organization or website may provide or recommendations it may make. Further, readers should be aware that internet websites listed in this work may have changed or disappeared between when this work was written and when it is read.

ISBN 978-1-61448-851-4 paperback
ISBN 978-1-61448-852-1 hard cover
ISBN 978-1-61448-854-5 eBook
Library of Congress Control Number: 2013945997

Morgan James Publishing
The Entrepreneurial Publisher
5 Penn Plaza, 23rd Floor,
New York City, New York 10001
(212) 655-5470 office • (516) 908-4496 fax
www.MorganJamesPublishing.com

Co-Edited by:
Mandi Vanek and
Natalie M. Wheeler

Cover Design by:
Rachel Lopez
www.r2cdesign.com

Interior Design by:
Bonnie Bushman
bonnie@caboodlegraphics.com

In an effort to support local communities, raise awareness and funds, Morgan James Publishing donates a percentage of all book sales for the life of each book to Habitat for Humanity Peninsula and Greater Williamsburg.

Get involved today, visit
www.MorganJamesBuilds.com.

Habitat
for Humanity®
Peninsula and
Greater Williamsburg
Building Partner

CONTENTS

ACKNOWLEDGEMENTS

I would like thank all the brilliant authors who have shared their stories in this volume. Their dedication to following their passion and delivering value to others is inspiring to me. The better I get to know each of you, the more your light shines!

To my friends and family, thanks for your continued support and belief in me. I confess that I can't even keep up with the plates I am spinning, so I don't expect you to.

Special thanks are due to my assistant, Natalie, for all she has done to help pull this massive effort together. Who knew herding cats could be so much fun?

Recognition is deserved for my friend, David Hancock, and his fantastic team at Morgan James Publishing. You are part of the new publishing revolution and I'm proud to be on this journey with you.

I'd like to give a reluctant nod to Sprite, who invariably finds the worst time to slink across my keyboard while I am in mid-edit, but does it in such a way that I can't help but stroke her furry tail.

And most of all, this book is dedicated to the genius next door and your commitment to doing the thing that makes you tick. Whether or not anyone knows just how brilliant you are at what you do, keep doing it. You DO make a difference.

INTRODUCTION

By Joel Comm

With eager anticipation, you enter the networking event hoping you will meet new people. Armed with business cards, pressed clothes and a genuine smile, you are prepared to walk away with new connections.

Upon entering the room, your eyes meet the eyes of a stranger. They, too, are there for one reason. Networking.

Knowing this stranger is about to become an acquaintance, you approach them with a "hello, my name is…." accompanied by a firm handshake. They reply with their name and "It's nice to meet you!"

The words that follow proceed from their lips as the question most frequently asked at events such as this. You can hear the words in your head before they are even uttered… "So, what do YOU do?"

With elevator speech already rehearsed in your mind, you proceed to share your story.

And that's what it's really about, isn't it? Your story.

You see, I firmly believe that everyone has a story to tell. Now not everyone is telling their story, and many of us are in the process of writing our story. But for the most part, we can all say that we've "been there, done that" in some respect. We have a story to tell.

While the story doesn't necessarily define who we are, in all likelihood it comes from a significant place inside us. That's because our story is most often the result of who we have become and what we have experienced.

I'm of the mindset that everyone who walks the face of earth has been created by God with passions, talents, skills, abilities, personality and presence, all of which whose combination is what makes us entirely unique. Who we are is so unique that there has never been a person just like us, nor will there ever be one.

Because we are uniquely designed, one may conclude that each one of us brings a unique value to the world around us. I'm not talking about our value as human beings. Certainly, we all have intrinsic value just because we are human.

I'm referring to the value we bring through the passions which drive of from our beds in the morning, the talents which help us to stand out from the crowd, the skills which we have honed through the crucible of experience, the abilities which cause others to pay attention to us, the personality that defines how others experience us and the presence that says "I am here and I matter!"

The value we bring has the potential to not only affect, but to change, other people's lives. I'm talking about YOU, now. The value YOU bring has the potential to change the course of your family, your community, your city or state, your country and the world.

Yes, you are that significant. And what you do, how you do it and why you do what you do are all very important.

We live in a celebrity culture. We tend to elevate those who achieved some degree of recognition above the rest of us.

I'm not saying there isn't value in learning from a New York Times best-selling author, supporting a passionate politician or seeking to emulate the path of a successful businessperson.

But when you think about the most remarkable people you know, aren't they people that you actually know?

Where do you find the greatest passion? Who is truly impacting your world?

I think you'll agree that it is your children's teachers, the volunteers at the homeless shelter in your community, the local band that plays at the summer fair, the civil engineers that make your roads safe, the baker who creates delicious treats, the fireman who risk their lives daily, and the countless other people in your neighborhood, who are truly the heroes that surround you every day. Their passion, talents, skills, ability, personality and presence permeate your realm to bring a never-ending stream of value to your life and to the lives of those around you.

I would assert that there is far more wisdom in the unsung heroes of your world than there is in the people we place on pedestals.

Yes, there is genius surrounding you. And that genius may be next door.

This book is a book of stories; stories from people like you and me; people with something to say. Each one has been chosen because of the unique value they bring to the world around them.

Whether focused on relational topics such as becoming a better spouse or parent, technical topics dealing with design or the law, or creative topics such as music and the arts, the individuals in this book are passionate. They have something to say, and they have value which they desire to bring to your world.

The forty-six authors within will excite you as you discover the breadth and depth of their passion and knowledge. Whether coming from a physical or a spiritual perspective, they will inspire you to look at the world a little differently. And perhaps they will challenge you to come out from your own personal comfort zone, either by gently pulling you into their world, or by causing you to take a closer look at the value you are bringing, or wish to bring, to those around you.

"So, what do you do?" is a simple question. But behind the question is a passionate person wanting to shout their story from the rooftop in hopes of impacting their world.

I hope these stories impact you in a positive way. Join me as we discover the genius next door.

FREE MEMBERSHIP!

Claim Your Free Membership, Bonuses and an Opportunity to Be Featured in a Future Volume of "So, What Do YOU Do?", for book buyers only!

Joel Comm and the So What Do You Do Authors would like to present you free access to a number of free bonuses which are yours for the asking. As a book buyer, you are eligible to receive free reports, audios, videos and memberships related to the expertise of a number of the authors within.

Would you like your story to appear in a future volume of So What Do You Do? If you are an expert in your field, you may apply to be considered for a chapter! To claim your bonuses and find an application to be included in a future volume, go to:

SoWhatDoYouDo.com

SLUM DOC VISIONAIRE
by Ashish Goyal

The heat, humidity, and smell of garbage were starting to get to me. It was my last day working in India as a volunteer medical student in one of the largest slums in the world, Dharavi. The Niramaya Health Foundation had started a makeshift clinic in the Mumbai area, which has since been popularized by the movie "Slumdog Millionaire." The clinic offered medical care to locals, including a large population of illegal child-laborers. The day had been fairly uneventful until a 12-year-old boy was brought in by his sweatshop employer. He had the chills and looked like he was about to collapse. I examined him and noticed that he was dehydrated, running a high fever, breathing fast, and coughing repeatedly. I heard the crackling sounds of pneumonia in his lungs and his heartbeat was faster than I could count. I started asking him questions about how he was feeling, but he kept telling me he felt fine. I could tell he was nervous, and then I realized that his employer was standing directly behind him, listening to every word.

I approached the clinic doctor with my diagnosis and recommended that the boy be hospitalized. Dr. Amit shared my concerns but explained to me that the sweatshop employers were just starting to trust us, and making such a drastic recommendation would work against the child's best interests. He said that the employer would simply leave and take the child to a clinic that "knows" what they're doing, or worse, take him back to the sweatshop and deal with the problem later.

I told him at the very least we needed to prescribe some hard-hitting antibiotics, provide direction on how to keep him hydrated, and make sure we follow up. Dr. Amit told me that the clinic didn't stock those antibiotics, and "outside medicines" cost money that the employers are not willing to spend—employers come to the clinic because they know it's free.

Just as I had started to convince myself that we were making progress, and that four years of medical school had prepared me for this moment, Dr. Amit's comments reminded me of the realities of slum life in Dharavi. I had seen poverty and poor health during that month, but this was a life and death situation. I found myself pleading with Dr. Amit, but it seemed there was no good alternative.

On the flight back to the U.S. that night, I couldn't stop thinking about my experiences as a Niramaya volunteer. How could the situation be so dire that a child with life-threatening pneumonia actually sees a doctor and still can't get the care he needs? I knew there had to be more that I could do than put the experience behind me.

Seven months later I returned to India. Something inside me had been ignited, and I decided to put the remainder of my medical training on hold for a year. I returned to India with a three-fold mission. First, help Niramaya improve their existing clinics. Second, assist them in starting a new, modernized clinic. And finally, I'd recruit one volunteer per month in order to ensure the volunteer effort remained stable after I left. I worked 15-20 hours per day, doubting all of this was even possible. To my own surprise, by the fifth month I had improved Niramaya's existing clinics, started an adolescent health and sex education program, and helped Niramaya open a new, modernized clinic in a slum community desperate for healthcare. The clinic treated over 70 child sweatshop laborers on its first day, and an estimated 2,000 people over the next 12 months. Eventually, the clinic was relocated to a larger facility due to overwhelming demand.

While some of my accomplishments during those five months required medical knowledge, I noticed that most of the value I was providing wasn't due to my medical training at all. It was my willingness to help wherever there was a need. For example, there were no electronic records of the patient forms being used, so I replicated the documents in Word and made some modifications based on Dr. Amit's recommendations. I also assisted in designing a unique patient record keeping system and suggested placing a wooden partition between the examination and waiting areas to safeguard the patients' privacy and reduce the background noises that were interfering with heart and lung exams. These changes didn't require complex medical knowledge, they required someone who was passionate about "helping where help was needed."

I still had six months left and the most difficult task ahead: help Niramaya recruit one volunteer per month after I left. My desire to accomplish this goal was fueled by the poverty that surrounded me. People lived on top of garbage dumps, didn't have toilets, and couldn't afford basic medical care. My accomplishments had given me the confidence to think big, and I decided to start my own nonprofit organization. I didn't want to reinvent the wheel, I merely wanted to help it roll faster.

I named the organization AVSAR. Its mission was to find passionate volunteers to work with grassroots organizations in an effort to enhance existing programs and create new ones, both of which would survive long after I left. In other words, "help where help was needed." During the pilot stage, I recruited six volunteers for four different nonprofit organizations, including Niramaya. They embraced AVSAR's mission and were more creative in their efforts than I could have ever imagined.

When I returned to the U.S. at the end of the year, I left a local staff to run the program. There were also many volunteers willing to contribute a program fee in return for support and guidance. They were MBA students, doctors, dentists, engineers, web designers, college students, teachers, and others who simply wanted to make a difference. The AVSAR personnel welcomed them at the airport, housed them, provided computers, internet access, cell phones, food service, and even a two day orientation that covered volunteerism, the city, transportation, and cultural barriers. AVSAR aimed to remove all obstacles so that volunteers could focus on one thing: making an impact.

Within a few years, AVSAR hosted over 100 volunteers from over ten countries. My one-month experience as a volunteer had turned into over a decade of service that touched tens of thousands of lives. Although the organization was doing great work, I had started AVSAR with $20,000 of my own money. As the organization's potential grew, it was limited by my money and time. I was unable to hire a CEO or help scale it because I was working 80 hours per week as a medical intern. Unable to give the organization the attention it deserved, I chose to suspend operations until I could come up with a solution.

In 2011, I started a company called PediatricsBoardReview.com (PBR). Through PBR I've helped pediatricians from around the world pass their medical board exams. The income has allowed me to work on a part-time basis and pursue my passion for making a difference on a greater scale. I've donated an additional $50,000 to AVSAR and plan to raise another $50,000-$100,000 for its re-launch.

It's exciting to think of everything the new AVSAR will do for the world. The need is tremendous, and AVSAR's potential to become the center of a network of nonprofit organizations will have a global impact. Through the hard work of so many AVSAR Alumni, it's obvious that anyone can help make a difference if they are simply willing to "help where help is needed."

To learn more about how you can help where help is needed, simply visit www.AvsarVolunteers.org/help.

ABOUT THE AUTHOR

 **Dr. Ashish Goyal** is a double board-certified physician, an entrepreneur, and a pioneer in the field of philanthropy. Ashish's passion for making a difference on a greater scale and his experiences in social entrepreneurship, volunteer management, and problem solving led to the creation of AvsarVolunteers.org, a nonprofit organization focused on empowering grassroots organizations in poverty-stricken cities through international volunteer support, technology, and improved infrastructure.

Ashish is also the CEO of PediatricsBoardReview.com (PBR), a company which helps pediatricians from around the world pass their medical board exams. To date, PBR has funded AVSAR with over $50,000. To become inspired by AVSAR, visit www.AvsarVolunteers.org.

facebook.com/AvsarVolunteers

twitter.com/AvsarVolunteers

www.linkedin.com/company/avsar

LESSONS IN T-BALL

by Ted Prodromou

I t's the bottom of the 9th inning. The score is 4-3 and the bases are loaded. The count is full and the cleanup hitter has fouled off four pitches in a row. A walk will tie the game. A base hit and we lose.

Our catcher calls time-out and jogs to the mound to strategize with our pitcher. They're trying to figure out how to get this guy out. After a quick chat, they give each other a nod—the plan is in place. Our pitcher takes a deep breath and steps onto the mound. He looks to the catcher for the sign. He winds up and throws a change-up that totally fools the batter. Strike out! We are the champions of the San Anselmo Baseball Association again!

Yes, this is a story about Little League Baseball; about how a brother and sister with no experience coached their sons to three championships in four years against rival coaches who played college baseball.

But this narrative is much more than a story about how to win Little League championships. As the years pass, I realize the significant impact we had on those eight to twelve year olds. We taught them life lessons that affected their lives as well as ours. Kids often get frustrated when they strike out or can't catch a hard hit ball. You fail most of the time in baseball, so you have to learn how to pick yourself up, dust off the disappointment, and get back into the game. I often see the boys (now men) around town and they always thank me for those great seasons. Countless parents tell me how we changed their kids' lives by teaching them not only how to play baseball but how to be confident and overcome their fear of failure.

Do you want to know the secret of our success?

Our success wasn't planned. It's not like my sister and I sat down one day and devised a strategy to dominate the local Little League. It was purely an accident that we won so many championships. Actually, looking back on our experience, maybe it wasn't an accident after all.

The other coaches' experience turned out to be a competitive advantage. My sister Connie and I stopped playing Little League when we were teenagers (she still plays co-ed softball today in her late 50's) and knew nothing about coaching baseball, which also turned out to be an advantage.

The other coaches focused on teaching advanced drills to their teams. They used to put the kids through the same drills they practiced when they played high school and college ball. One coach even had a playbook that the kids had to memorize in order to play on his team. He taught them numerous defensive formations and would bark out code names during the games. The kids would instantly jump into the proper defensive formation. It looked impressive, but it didn't win them many games!

Connie and I had a completely opposite approach. We realized that most of these kids had never played baseball. Most of them could barely throw or catch and only a few could hit the ball. We focused on teaching the fundamentals of baseball: how to throw, catch and swing properly. Our expectations were very different from those of the other coaches.

This is basically what our roster looked like each season:

- One or two boys were really good and were appointed the team leaders.
- Eight to ten boys had a little baseball experience; they could throw and catch but not very well.

- The rest of the team could barely catch or throw. If they got a hit during a game it was because the pitch accidentally hit the bat.

While the other coaches spent most of their time working with the top five or six players on the team, Connie and I focused on the bottom ten. We knew the kids who were already good would get better just by coming to practice and playing games. We worked with them a little in practice to help them improve, but most of our time was spent teaching the others how to throw, catch, and swing the bat properly.

My expectations for the bottom half of the team were simple: If they caught one fly ball or fielded a grounder during the season it was a successful season. If they got one hit during the season, I was ecstatic. You see, if one of the weaker players on the team made one play, whether in the field or at bat, we usually won the game.

I concentrated on building the confidence of the weakest players. My only rule was that they always tried their hardest. If they erred in the field or struck out at bat but gave it their all, I was fine with it. If they didn't try their hardest, I would push them to give 100% at all times. I didn't expect perfection, but I did expect their best efforts.

Oh yeah, I also encouraged them to have fun. The other coaches were so absorbed with winning while we were having the time of our lives. Baseball is a game isn't it? Games are supposed to be fun!

The result?

Each year I coached, every player on the team had at least one hit. I remember one game in which the bases were loaded and there were two outs. The boy coming up to bat had never played baseball and hadn't come close to getting a hit that season. He was trembling as he walked up to the plate because he was afraid of making the last out. I called time-out so I could talk to him and calm him down.

First I told him to take a few deep breaths to relax. Then I asked him what he really loved doing and what he felt comfortable doing. He said, "I'm a great skier," so I told him to imagine himself on the slopes, flying down the hill. He instantly lit up and stood tall. He walked up to the plate with a big smile on his face and more confident than I had ever seen him. He hit a single and was the hero of the game. To this day, we both remember that moment.

So what's the moral of this story?

Life can be very complicated. Keep it simple and enjoy every minute like it's your last.

My Little League coaching experience is just one of many stories from my life. I was born with the gift of simplifying the complex. I love mentoring others; I'm constantly helping people simplify their complexities so they can live their lives to the fullest.

ABOUT THE AUTHOR

An author, consultant, and expert in online advertising, social media, lead generation, and search engine optimization, **Ted Prodromou** helps small to medium-sized companies increase their profits and expand their global presence on the Internet.

Utilizing the latest techniques, including social media, podcasting, online advertising, video, blogging, and Google AdWords, Ted transforms run-of-the-mill websites into successful ventures.

Ted is a regular contributor to Entrepreneur.com and penned the articles, Ultimate Guide to Linked in for Business: How to Get Connected with 150 Million Customers in 10 Minutes and Ultimate Guide to Twitter for Business for Entrepreneur Magazine's "Ultimate Guide" series. His low-cost social media strategies have helped companies of all sizes reach more customers and grow their businesses.

To learn more about how Ted can help you grow your business visit tedprodromou.com.

facebook.com/tedprodromou

twitter.com/tedprodromou

linkedin.com/in/tedprodromou

MY MOTHER WAS RIGHT

by Connie Ragen Green

I grew up extremely poor. My mother's answer for securing my financial future was education. It was just the two of us, and from the time I was in elementary school, every weekend we would take the bus to one of the colleges or universities in the Los Angeles area. When I was twelve we moved to Miami and our campus tours continued there. While we were visiting these institutions of higher learning, my mom would talk about what my life would be like as a college student. She told me that I could do anything I wanted to with my life. I now understand my mother's thinking at the time, but it did discourage me from embracing my entrepreneurial desires.

The summer I turned thirteen I started two businesses. One was a babysitting service with some of my girlfriends, and the other was a lawn mowing service with the boy next door. Mom reluctantly allowed me to do this, but was much happier in the fall when our neighbor offered me a weekend job as a hostess at the restaurant he managed. I worked there every Saturday and Sunday for almost a year, until his daughter came back from college and needed the job.

The following summer I went back to creating my own income, this time raising salt water fish and gerbils to sell to the local pet store and scraping barnacles off of boats. At this young age I could already see the benefits of owning a business: flexible hours, the ability to earn more money when you needed it, and no worries about being replaced by the manager's daughter.

But my mother's influence eventually won out, and so I decided to go to college and study veterinary medicine. In high school I took a job at an animal clinic, learning as much as I could about the profession. My life then began to take many twists and turns, and I finally decided that the pain and suffering of the animals was too much for me to bear. After graduating from college I went on to law school for a year, worked as a claims adjuster, and finally became a real estate agent.

My twenties were unremarkable, and around age thirty I decided I needed something more out of my life. When the Challenger Space Shuttle disaster occurred in January, 1986, I thought about my childhood dream of becoming a classroom teacher. Immediately after the Challenger tragedy, the media focused on the students at Christa McAuliffe's school and I saw in their eyes what this teacher, who would have become the first teacher in space, had meant to them. Within a year I was enrolled in a teaching certification program and working in my neighborhood school as a teaching assistant. For the first time in my life I felt like the work I was doing was meaningful.

Fast forward twenty years. I'd worked as a classroom teacher in four different schools, teaching kindergarten through high school (I liked fifth graders the most). Teachers do not earn a ton of money, so I had been selling real estate all those years so I could own a home and take a vacation every other year. This meant leaving my house before six each morning to beat the rush hour traffic on the way to school, finishing by four or so, and then going on to my real estate appointments. My weekends, holidays, and breaks were spent working the real estate market. And did I mention that I also had cancer three times during all of this?

Along the way I volunteered as a Big Sister to a disabled African-American girl and was a foster mother to a boy from a dysfunctional family. Other than that I did little to give back to my community or the world. As I got older it became glaringly apparent to me that unless something changed, this would be the story of my life. At that point, however, I was still taking a passive role, waiting for someone else to make things happen for me.

I woke up one day and decided it was time to take full responsibility for my life and take actions that would initiate change. My fiftieth birthday was approaching and I was ready to transform my life. It was as though something had stirred inside me for the first time in many years, and I was ready to move on to the next phase. I began a quest for knowledge, devouring books and listening to CDs in my car. This went on for six months, until I finally heard that people were running businesses entirely from their computer, creating and selling informational products.

This idea resonated with me and soon I was devoting every spare moment I had to educating myself about how I could also become an online entrepreneur. One day I earned twenty-one dollars and sixty cents in commission from the sale of an eBook and I knew I could duplicate that process over and over again.

In June of 2006 I resigned from the school district, cashing out my retirement account and taking responsibility for my own health insurance. I knew I would miss teaching, but I felt as if I had no choice. Simultaneously, I gave my real estate clients to others who could better serve their needs. I knew I would also miss helping people in this way, but again I felt I had to take this step. Burning my bridges was scary, but not doing it at this point in my life seemed even more frightening. It was a leap of faith, and I was hurdling myself into it at full speed.

The first year was a struggle, but I loved the idea of creating my own destiny. This was also a time of self- realization. When someone on my tiny email list asked me to explain something to them I realized I was a teacher again! The truth was that I would always be a teacher, and this was yet another way to share my knowledge with others and help them achieve their goals.

I'm currently in my seventh year as an online entrepreneur, and I cannot imagine doing anything else for the remainder of my life. I've forged relationships with people from around the globe and achieved goals I had previously only dreamed of. My online community looks to me for guidance in creating informational products, setting up membership sites, increasing credibility and visibility, and writing blogs and even books. I'm truly making a difference in their lives.

My mother was right—I was able to do whatever I wanted with my life, and the lessons I've learned from this are that you must take that leap of faith in order to do what your heart and soul are telling you to do, and that sharing your knowledge and experiences with others can be a gift and a blessing, to them and to you. And most importantly, I'm a teacher once again!

ABOUT THE AUTHOR

 **Connie Ragen Green** is an award-winning author and international speaker who has helped people on six continents become online entrepreneurs. A former classroom teacher and real estate appraiser, she left it all behind in 2006 to launch an online business. Although she struggled during her first year, Connie remained determined to put the pieces together and become a successful entrepreneur. Upon accomplishing her goal, Connie vowed to dedicate her life to teaching others how to leverage the power of the Internet to create the lifestyle of their dreams.

facebook.com/ConnieRagenGreen

twitter.com/ConnieGreen

www.linkedin.com/in/connieragengreen/

TRAVELING AROUND THE WORLD

by Sheila Simkin

W hile growing up, my mother read books to me about "Chilly Willy the Penguin" who floated on his ice flow from Antarctica to a tropical island, "Ferdinand the Bull" who lived in Spain, and "The Five Little Peppers" who traveled through Europe with Grandpapa. I too wanted to travel the world, although the ice flow sounded scary. My mother had a different opinion. Her broken record refrain was, "When you grow up and get married, you can go wherever you want, but as long as you live under my roof, forget it!"

And so it happened. Marriage! Upon that "happy" occasion, the first thing I did on my honeymoon was coax my husband to abandon Miami Beach for Cuba in 1960! Fidel Castro had come into power and Cuba was practically paying tourists to visit. That was it—the world beckoned and Sheila had to explore. If it meant dragging babies on red eye flights, sitting in airports overnight, traveling offseason, scrimping, plotting and planning, and even dragging my four-year old door to door with me while I took surveys, so be it. As I became more adventurous, my sons Michael and Joel learned to ski in Colorado, we cruised on ships that have subsequently sunk to the bottom of the sea, and even gutted out a long distance flight to London.

My marriage eventually dissolved (my ex-husband was probably thrilled as he never did like to travel), and in 1977 I remarried. When my husband Steve and I were dating, I asked him if he liked to travel, to which he replied, "I love Mexico and Las Vegas." Little did the poor man know what I had in mind...a one month trip to Europe with five children, aged 9-16, in tow. We stayed in small pensions and schlepped luggage on and off trains during this nightmare of a trip. Steve chased children up and down foreign streets, threatening to kill one of them. And the dynamics were insufferable: Four children against one, two against three, two against two, boys against girls. It's no wonder Steve chain smoked while screaming he hated them all. Tracie (14) sulked over missing parties back home, Robbie (13) and Joel (13) got food poisoning in Florence, and Robbie added her own touch by throwing up spaghetti in a sink, almost creating an international incident as Italian maids ran back and forth trying to unclog the drain. Ugh... The grand finale took place in a Roman restaurant when a family member provoked a loud crying, screaming, and swearing match in front of horror-stricken locals. If a person can survive that, they can do anything!

With over 50 years of unique and "normal" travel experiences under my belt, friends and acquaintances constantly nagged me for travel advice and information. "What's your favorite country...How do you get from Charles de Gaulle Airport to Paris...Do I need inoculations... Can I wear blue jeans...Will I get kidnapped in Egypt..." and so on. In the meantime, searching for potential travel information on the Net was driving me crazy! Have you ever conducted an extensive Google search only to find pages filled with ads and no information?

A void of reliable travel information pushed me kicking and screaming into the blogosphere, and I created TravelsWithSheila.com with one goal in mind: To encourage fellow travelers to take the big step and visit exotic, remote destinations by providing tips, anecdotes, and reassurances that, yes, they will come back **alive**. Many people would like to travel internationally but aren't sure how to go about it and are under the illusion that only millionaires can afford this luxury thanks to magazines like Travel & Leisure and Conde Nast Traveller.

Travel writing is not for the faint-hearted and it took seven years of hard work before I was able to make a name for myself in this industry. I learned to film and edit videos and write more cohesively as travel slowly became a lifelong addiction. For a person who never owned a camcorder and often traveled **without** a camera hanging around her neck, this was a major learning process. But just look at me now!

Over 1,500 videos have been uploaded to YouTube.com on the "travelswithsheila" channel. Filmed around the world, they cover the gamut: taking a cruise; camping in a desert in Egypt; street, restaurant, and local cuisine (fried tarantulas, anyone?); cultural and tribal sights; and even instructions on how to navigate public transportation in Paris, Beijing, Istanbul, Bangkok, Singapore, Kiev, and other world cities.

Next came the Travels With Sheila Guides on both Kindle and Create that tell the whole truth about each country and whether the sights and attractions are a hit or a miss. Follow my advice to avoid learning travel lessons the hard way. For example, **do you know:**

- An **air mattress** is necessary for camping and trekking? A never to be forgotten week spent in a sleeping bag on the cold, hard ground of Nepal with no protection taught us that.
- Only crazy idiots go trekking and get lost in Siberia. **Really?** The Siberian horseman who was supposed to wait for us decided his horse was getting tired and left. To make things worse, it would have cost less money to be imprisoned in a Siberian gulag with the same discomfort.
- How to use a "hole in the ground" toilet without **soiling** yourself and/or the surrounding area? That was one messy learning experience.
- No country in the world will accept a **Xerox copy** or other **replica** of your passport? (Including the United States.) Who else but Sheila forgets an old passport with a still valid 10

year India visa at home? I was instantly "repatriated" from the Delhi, India airport. Oh, let's tell it like it is—I was **thrown** out of the country.

- How to play the airline mileage game? What to use miles for? Which are the best credit cards for travel? An ATM card is the best friend you will ever have while traveling?

I am not a travel agent, have no affiliation with any agency or airline, and tell it as I see it. However, I have developed non-commissionable associations with many good and reasonable tour operators who I connect my readers withTravelsWithSheila.com is not directed at backpackers (although they do read the articles and watch the videos) or extremely wealthy travelers who want to stay in only the best hotels, fly first class, and book suites on cruise ships. Any travel agent will be happy to assist with these arrangements. After all, it's a no-brainer to book a room at the Ritz Carlton or Four Seasons Hotel (not that there is anything wrong with that; I adore five-star hotels). But I am a **pro** at making travel money stretch into infinity and beyond.

If you want to travel and are willing to put up with the occasional discomfort (after all, travel is never perfect), you CAN do it on a budget! I enjoy writing articles and filming videos that will get people there and back without paragraphs of hyperbole extolling turquoise waters ringing the infinity pool. If you're interested in reading about rainy seasons and box jellyfish that will kill a person, I invite you to journey with me. Happy traveling!

ABOUT THE AUTHOR

Sheila Simkin, a native Chicagoan, is a travel addict who has been exploring the world since 1960. There are few countries that are not on her to-see list, no matter how remote and/or difficult to get to. The US State Department recognizes 193 independent countries and she has visited 130 over 50 years (but who's counting?).

TravelsWithSheila.com delivers the cold hard truth about everything travel related and provides tips for stretching a travel budget. From touring, hiking, trekking, rafting, snowshoeing, skiing, volunteering on an archaeological dig, and taking family trips to sitting on a beach and compulsively shopping, Sheila has probably been there and done it. Visit www.TravelsWithSheila.com to follow all of Sheila's travels and tips.

www.facebook.com/sheila.simkin.3

twitter.com/sheilatravels

www.linkedin.com/pub/sheila-simkin/1b/841/612

PAY IT FORWARD

by Patricia Clason

I was told I had two choices: start over in a new body or go back into my current body. Either way, I had to do the work I was meant to do on this earth. I looked down at my body from the upper corner of the hospital room; it wasn't breathing and it wasn't moving. I knew my body had died.

I didn't want to start all over again, so I chose to continue in my current body and headed back. The next thing I remember was waking up in the hospital bed unable to move. I could only project sound in the form of screams from the pain that rendered me unconscious. I later found out that I had experienced a near death experience, caused by a combination of too many drugs and an extreme allergic reaction to the anesthetic needed for a procedure the doctor ordered. After months of being on high doses of pain medicine, I was able to slowly wean off the medication, and as my mind began to clear, I knew that I had to learn how to heal myself, not only on a physical level but more importantly, an emotional level. I knew I needed to do something more with the life I was blessed with.

The emotions that I had numbed with the drugs started to surface, but instead of suppressing them, I decided to face them head on. I wrote down my feelings and over time developed a system of journaling that worked for me. I started attending and getting involved in personal growth seminars and learned two very important concepts. It all came together for me and those two fundamental basics are now the underpinning of my life.

The first concept is personal responsibility. I had to stop blaming the government, my parents, society, and anyone else for my circumstances. I had to learn response-ability and find my strength in it. I learned that taking responsibility for my feelings and thoughts and what I do with them is actually a very fulfilling way of living. I am in charge of who I am, what I feel, what I do, and what I create in life. With this mindset, when life starts to go haywire I can take action, make changes, and build the life I want to live. It wasn't easy. Forty years ago we didn't have the resources we do today. We didn't have the Internet, and people didn't go to therapists or "shrinks." I often felt like I was on my own, but I was fortunate to find help along the way.

The second concept is the free expression of emotions. As I traveled down my new path, I found that how I channeled my emotions was a critical aspect of my well-being. When I pushed emotion down, ignored, or denied it, I would later explode and cause a messy argument or go into a depression. When I allowed emotion to flow freely and expressed it in a healthy way, I could use that energy-in-motion to make things happen, build deeper relationships, and enjoy my daily life.

Two very basic concepts, sometimes challenging to practice, yet when integrated into one's life, make everyday living satisfying, rewarding, and successful. Along the way, someone made a comment to me about "teaching what one most needs to learn." What I needed to learn was how to enjoy my life, regardless of how much money I did or didn't have, how many people were or were not around me, or what the weather was like outside. I decided to take what I was learning and teach it to others. I could do this authentically because I didn't claim to have all the answers, make you rich overnight, or help you find the perfect relationship that would give you bliss for the rest of your life. I simply shared the basic concepts that I practice every day and my trial and error experiences, so others didn't make the same mistakes I did (although sometimes people did because they had to learn the hard way).

After many years of practicing what I teach, I still experience setbacks and obstacles. A divorce at fifty cracked my foundation—it was unexpected and devastating! So I returned to the basics. I wrote every day. In the morning, I set an intention for the day. I decided what gift I would give to myself to celebrate my worth. One day it was flowers, another day steaming chai from my favorite coffee shop or leaving myself a message on the answering machine about how courageous and loving I am. Every evening, I wrote my gratitude for the day, acknowledging all of the successes, no matter how small, and all of the good I experienced. It took a year (I still have ALL of the pages) for me to feel steady and strong again. It wasn't dramatic or quick, but it was deep and powerful. I had rebuilt a strong foundation for my life that could support me during any storm.

The basics are often forgotten with the rate of change, the expectation that we should produce big, fancy results, or the need to simply survive. I have met people with very little who are full of joy and appreciation for life. They love their families and are grateful for what they have, and they don't focus on what they lack. So whatever you do, if life isn't fulfilling, satisfying, or successful, I'm here to remind you that "back to the basics" is the way to go. I enjoy sharing the "Five Laws of Wealth" that helped me find financial stability. I also provide communication basics that helps people create functional relationships at home and at work. My delight is in guiding people in restoring integrity and accountability so they can take charge of their world and accomplish their goals and dreams. All of this comes from my knowledge and experience, not someone else's theory.

I also encourage people to "Pay It Forward," to give in gratitude for what you have received. Whether it's change you leave at the cash register for the next person, time you share with someone who needs help with their yard work or a project, or a donation to a charity, giving back is essential. I look at it this way: love is flow, giving is receiving. The benefits of helping another are immense, for them and for you.

My most important 'pay it forward' is the work I do in a veterans retreat called Healing Warrior Hearts. It is free to veterans, which is my way (and the way of many others who are involved) of saying thank you for fighting for this country and our freedom. My life's mission is saving hearts. I share the experiences, lessons, and basics that helped me find my joy again so that you will be able to fully open your heart to life. It's the best possible gift I could give you, and the best way I can say thank you for the amazing life I get to live. Enjoy your ride!

ABOUT THE AUTHOR

Patricia Clason uses her talent for communicating to positively impact lives. She's authored and implemented over fifty training programs, including the "Claim Your Unlimited Potential" series and "Speaking of Success" (with Stephen Covey, Jack Canfield, and Ken Blanchard), and has hosted and been a guest on numerous radio and television programs. Patricia speaks, trains, and coaches those who are searching for emotional intelligence. Her own path of healing has given her a special empathy for others' journeys. You may find Patricia's writings at: patriciaclason.com (corporate training), lightly.com (personal growth), or healingwarriorhearts.org (retreats for veterans).

facebook.com/patricia.clason
twitter.com/EQCoachClason
www.linkedin.com/in/patriciaclason

THE DULL MEN'S CLUB
by Leland Carlson

irport luggage carousels have fascinated me for years. I like to watch the bags going around. At first I thought it was because I'm a model railroader and the bags and carousels reminded me of my trains and tracks.

But then I saw a deeper meaning. When I get to my destination, get off the airplane and head to the baggage area, I'm walking with a sense of anticipation—looking forward to picking up my bag and getting on with my trip. There's also a sense of fear—what if the bag's not there? My bag usually arrives, however—and wow—what a joyful feeling that is.

This repeats itself when I return home. The joyful feeling of seeing my bag again. A fine ending to the trip.

As the years went on, I began to notice that not all luggage carousels were alike. Some rotated clockwise, others rotated counterclockwise. I started a list.

The list, as it grew, revealed that the majority of the carousels, over 2/3's, went counterclockwise. I didn't know the reason why this was the case, until recently.

Some years later, airport luggage carousels were a fitting topic for discussions at a club—the Dull Men's Club—I formed with some like-minded souls in New York.

We were sitting in the bar at the New York Athletic Club. We had finished our workouts (I had done my sit-up, I got all the way up, by myself) and were about to have dinner. We were reading the latest issue of the club's monthly magazine.

The magazine had articles about clubs-within-the-club: clubs for squash, tennis, judo, sailing, skiing. "We don't do any of those things," said one of the guys. "That's right, we're dull," said another. I said, "So let's start a page in the magazine for us dull men."

The magazine's publisher agreed. The Dull Men's Club was born.

Today the Dull Men's Club ("DMC") meets in cyberspace— dullmensclub.com—where we share ideas and experiences about simple, ordinary things. "Celebrate the Ordinary" has become the club's motto.

We avoid glitz and glam. We are not in-and-trendy. We avoid getting overly excited. Exclamation points are not allowed on our website, Facebook page, and tweets.

The DMC is not one of those twelve-step programs that try to change behavior. We are not trying to change. The DMC is a two-step program: (1) we admit we are dull; (2) we're going to keep it that way.

The DMC is not a "movement." We stay put.

There's a test to determine whether someone is eligible for DMC membership. The test's first two questions are: "Is gray one of your favorite colors?" "Have you ever had an urge—were you able to get over it?

I'm still associated with the DMC. My alter ego in the club, Grover Click, is assistant vice president—the DMC's highest office.

I'm retired from a real job now but am busier than ever. I divide my time among England (last place I worked), Washington, DC (worked there before England), and Chappell, Nebraska (hometown).

I could be fishing. Where I live in England, Winchester, I'm in the world's best trout fishing. In Nebraska I have a cabin on Nebraska's biggest lake, Lake McConaughy, also great for fishing.

But I'd rather do my fishing on the internet instead of in water. With Google as my fishing pole. I'd rather reel in an amusing item from the deep waters of the web than a fish.

I still get enthused when I find another new item that I think will interest dull men, such as:

- **Safe Excitement:** There's more to dull than watching paint dry. There's watching grass grow, snow melt, windshield wipers wipe, water freeze. And there's listening to corn grow, cement mixers mix, bubble wrap pop.

- **Appreciation Societies:** We join societies like the Cloud Appreciation Society, Apostrophe Protection Society, Biscuit Appreciation Society, Traffic Cone Preservation Society.

- **Collections and Museums:** We often avoid in-and-trendy exhibits at big-name museums, the ones with wine and cheese windings, and instead visit museums of ordinary objects, things like coat hangers, combs, gloves, manhole covers, banana stickers.

- **Races:** Fast and costly races like Formula 1, Indy 500, Kentucky Derby, Ascot are not for us. We get our adrenaline rushes from racing things like snails, turtles, ducks, library book carts.

- **Music:** Much of today's music is too exciting for us. In fact, we often prefer to listen to a metronome. It can be a traditional metronome, one on the Internet, or app for iPhone or Android. Lento is my favorite tempo, adagio once in a while, moderato on those rare occasions when I'm living it up.

- **Webcam Traveling:** now with webcams, we don't need to leave home—our serenity stations—to visit tourist attractions like the London Eye, Eiffel Tower, Red Square. We avoid having to pack and unpack, going through airport security, traffic jams. As for traffic jams, we can watch Jam Cams and see the agony we are avoiding.

- **Park Benches:** Park Benches: We love park benches. They are a true joy. We set up a Facebook group called the Park Bench

Appreciation Society. Park benches are places to take a break—sit down, watch the world go by. In fact, we often can cope with traveling to exciting cities so long as we can find park benches there. New York City is an example. Central Park is the Park Bench Capital of the World.

- Website Graveyard: We have a page where we pay tribute to websites we liked but have closed down. The leading example is the world's first webcam, Cambridge Coffee Pot Cam. Workers in the university's computer lab but far from the room with the lab's coffee pot set the webcam to see when coffee was ready. It was described as the Internet era's equivalent of Guttenberg's bible and Edison's light bulb. The coffee pot and webcam were unplugged, with appropriate funereal ceremony, when the lab moved to a new building in 2001. The coffee pot sold—auctioned off on the Internet of course—for $5,055.20.

The DMC has, I feel, a role to play today as much as it did when it was formed, probably even more so. Today I see people continuing to want more more more. More entertainment, more travel, more stuff. I call it "more-itis."

Does this make them more satisfied, more accomplished, happier? Usually not. Wouldn't they be OK if they simply enjoyed what they already have where they already are?

Much to its chagrin, the DMC has received publicity. It's attraction rather than promotion. It's like Field of Dreams, "If you build it, they will come."

In the U.S.:

- *The Wall Street Journal*: "Area Man Joins Organization Where Nothing Much Ever Happens" by Jennifer Levitz
- *The Boston Globe*: "Dull Men's Club celebrates the ordinary in Pembroke" by Emily Sweeney

- *NPR's Wait Wait... Don't Tell Me* "Bluff the Listener": three unlikely clubs were described, two were made up by the show's staff, one was not made up and that one was the DMC.

In the U.K.:

- *Reader's Digest*: "Best of British Clubs & Societies"—the DMC was included in the ten best clubs and societies, right up there with The Cloud Appreciation Society and The Pylon Appreciation Society.
- *Reuters*: "Enjoy watching grass grow? Join the dull men's club" by Sarah Ledwith.
- *The Sunday Times*: "Dusty Allure of the Dull Men's Club" by Roland White.
- BBC Two TV's *Mock the Week*: celebrity panel discusses the DMC's airport carousels report.

So what about the direction of airport luggage carousels? We now have reports for over 500 airports. Most continue to go counterclockwise. The most sensible reason (dull men like sensible), is because most people are right-handed, and right-handers have better balance and stability by reaching across to the left to pick up their bags. Dull men like balance and stability.

ABOUT THE AUTHOR

Leland V. Carlson ("Lee") is a senior who enjoys being senior. He divides his time now among England (last place he worked), Washington, DC (worked there before England), and Chappell, Nebraska (hometown)—and Colorado, California, and New York. He's a former tax attorney who now learns about computers, the internet, websites, blogging, and affiliate marketing. He has a website for the Dull Men's Club (www.dullmensclub.com—"Celebrating the Ordinary") and a website for seniors (www.seniorslaughing.com—"We didn't know there was so much for seniors to laugh at until we became one").

www.linkedin.com/profile/view?id=56641535

www.facebook.com/leland.carlson1

twitter.com/lelandcarlson

I AM NOT INVISIBLE!

by Arlene Krantz

"Mom, I want to be a nurse and I need to go to prep school to take the subjects I missed in high school." My mother's response was, "Arlene, why bother…you are only going to get married and have kids." My mother sure burst my nursing bubble.

So with my nursing dreams shattered, I became a secretary and a great one at that, but I knew that I wanted more in my life. I knew that I wanted to work my way up the ladder and become the president of a company someday. I used to dream about sitting in a big office behind a big desk running a big company. I could see it, feel it, and I wanted it.

Growing up I read a lot of biographies about successful people and could envision myself in their shoes. I came from humble beginnings; some days my father had money but most of the time he didn't. One day when I was about 11, I asked my father for money for an ice cream cone. He reached into his pocket and pulled out a $5.00 bill, which was all he had. I felt so guilty. "Dad, I really don't want the ice cream." He insisted. We had bill collectors calling and coming to our house and my two sisters and I had to lie and say our parents weren't home. I didn't realize then how much that effected my financial decisions. I was afraid to spend money because I knew what it was like not to have any and I made unhealthy decisions out of fear.

"I had just turned twenty, told me father I was getting married, and he said to me, "You haven't even lived yet." Of course I wasn't about to listen to him. I knew better, at least I thought I did. He was right. I didn't even have a chance to experience life and here I was getting married. My first daughter was born when I was 21 and the second when I was 23. I was a baby myself. I would sit with other mothers while our kids played and think to myself, "There has to be more to life than this." Talking about the latest appetizers and what to have for dinner was not for me. I read Time and Newsweek to find out what was happening in the world because my world was so small. I knew that my daughters would one day live their own lives and worried about what would be left for me.

I lost my voice early in my marriage. My husband ran everything I did by his mother and didn't listen to me at all. I was so depressed that one day I took an entire bottle of aspirin because I didn't want to live without a voice. I had so much to say and do and I felt like I was invisible. "Help, get me out of here!"

I still had the yearning to own a business and one day I told my husband that I wanted to open a bed and bath store. He looked at me like I was crazy and told me that I knew nothing about business and who did I think I was. Again, I shut down and lived my life according to what everyone else expected of me. Years later I divorced my husband and ended up working in a high end women's specialty store. I started out as a secretary and built a reputation as one who got things done, so when an opportunity to become an assistant buyer came my way I took it.

I had a fire inside of me and kept looking for opportunities to start a business. I had no money and my boyfriend had to help pay my rent. I would eat popcorn for dinner and when I invited friends over all I could afford was meatball-less spaghetti. But despite my financial distress, this was an incredible time for me. I worked four days a week and spent my free time developing a business plan. I was using credit cards to survive, but I was determined to be successful. An opportunity came my way and I couldn't say no. I borrowed money from friends and family. I needed $25,000 within a week and met a guy who believed in my business and loaned me the money.

When I talked to my mother, I told her how hard it was and her answer to me was, "If you had a secretary job, you wouldn't have to worry about making money." I told her not to call me if this is what she had to say, but I realized that she was worried about me so I didn't tell her or anyone else in my family anything about my plans after that conversation.

Nothing was going to stop me. I worked my butt off and grew my business from zero into a multi-million dollar company. I finally achieved what I always wanted to do. I loved the marketing, branding, advertising, and everything else I had learned from retail. I made it!

I had always loved giving business advice to people who had great business ideas and wondered if I could make money at it. I had never heard of a business coach and now I am one. You tell me your business and I'll tell you how to make money. I love helping people who want to start a business or grow their business. I love working with entrepreneurs and small business owners who are strong and courageous.

Julie is a genius with her camera. She wanted to grow her business and needed help. We positioned her as the go-to business photographer and now Julie's appointment book is full. I'm so proud of her and know that I made a difference in her life.

I met Manny at a Chamber meeting. He is the nicest guy but was also invisible because he didn't take a stand. People didn't really know what he did but after one week of working together he began building a business and had his first paying client within two weeks. Manny is now on the road to success. I always knew I had the ability to help others and now my voice is being heard.

In my book, The Business Within You, I provide 50 tips for turning your dream into a successful business. I talk about systems, social media, and thinking like a millionaire. It's amazing to me how many people who go into business have no clue about what they are doing or even the belief that they can do it. Have faith that it will happen and embrace your power with confidence and the world is yours.

This is about climbing the mountain to the top, have the business of your dreams, build a better world and help others bring peace to the planet.

ABOUT THE AUTHOR

Arlene Krantz is a speaker, author, and business coach. She is passionate about helping her clients grow their businesses and make the money they deserve. As an entrepreneur, she has over twenty-five years of experience and has grown her former business to over seven figures. She helps clients get clarity and overcome the obstacles that stop them from achieving their goals. She is a no nonsense coach who thinks out of the box while guiding her clients in their journey to fulfill their dreams and live a life of abundance.

If you would like more information on building a business, visit www.ArleneKrantz.com or email info@ArleneKrantz.com and put "So What Do You Do" on the subject line.

Here's to living a lifestyle of freedom and abundance.

facebook.com/arlenekrantz

twitter.com/arlenekrantz

lnkd.in/b5pZtE

THE IMPORTANCE OF MAKING A DIFFERENCE

by James D. Foster, Ph.D.

must have been in first grade; I was spending one of those fun weekends at work with my grandmother, Pearl Clickscales. I was very comfortable in the kitchen of that coach house situated above a six car garage. I was ready for another loving, fun-filled evening with a moon lit view of the big mansion off of Sheridan Road in Winnetka, IL. However, this night I had a very difficult time keeping my grandmother's attention. For some reason, she was paying more attention to the television than she was to me. I decided to figure out what could possibly be more important than her own grandchild. I intently watched as a flurry of activity seemed to be surrounding one man. I asked my grandmother, "Granny, why are they making such a big deal out of that man on T.V.?" She turned around with tears in her eyes and for the next two hours she explained to me the powerful significance of the Rev. Dr. Martin Luther King, Jr. It was April 4, 1968, the day MLK was assassinated. "Granny" would leave the comfort of her own home for the temporary working quarters of the coach house separated by a long driveway behind a mansion owned by W. Clement Stone, self-made millionaire and father of Positive Mental Attitude (PMA).

That night I learned from one significant influence (my Grandmother) about another significant and influential person (Dr. King). They have both left a powerful legacy that touched me personally. "Granny" is currently ninety-four years old; she taught me that even though life can be tough at times, with hard work and God's help there was absolutely nothing that I could not achieve. I was privileged to be raised by a supportive, loving family in a strong local faith community. I was taught the importance of making a difference, hard work, a dream, and the huge impact one pastor could make.

The next few years were filled with hope and the promise of a good life. I began my undercover career as a young man, traveling the country working corporate investigations. Needless to say, my adventures would probably make for a great book. It was during this time that I developed the necessary skills of personal relations, multi-dimensional observation, and credibility. My assignment, should I choose to accept it, was to establish a viable cover story and secure a position at the target company on my own. Once I was hired, I essentially had to work two jobs simultaneously, operating with strict integrity while completing detailed report writing, sometimes followed by hours of accurate unflappable testimony. I had to earn the trust of company employees while staying safe and alive.

The Importance of a Dream

During my last field assignment I was working a big drug case and living in Hunt Valley, a suburb of Baltimore, MD. I met a young lady on a break between assignments and we began dating. After some time, I began thinking about the possibilities of marriage and family, but my job was not exactly an ideal career for a married man with responsibilities at home. One night I arrived home late after a long day. After completing my reports, I fell asleep. I was awoken from a dream and heard what seemed like an audible voice. The instructions were: "Wake up and read Chapter 2 in the Book of Titus!" I jumped up, grabbed my Bible, and found Titus in the table of contents. The heading read, "Teach them." I later returned home to Bethel AME Church for guidance and an interpretation of this instruction. Although it wasn't easy, I was able to grow in faith and commitment.

A year after my last assignment ended, my wife Gerri Foster-Love and I were married in our home church by my pastor and mentor. Following the words in Titus, I held positions from teacher to district superintendent and later associate pastor. All of this took place while I was transitioning from undercover agent to office manager to leading sales manager, and eventually, partner.

The Call

I sold my interest in the agency to enroll in seminary college, recognizing and accepting that my calling in life was ministry. I worked in ministry while completing two seminary degrees and teaching at a major private university. The road was not easy. Ministry never is. However, it is exceedingly rewarding. Over the last two decades I have been blessed with a successful ministry and the pleasure of teaching others.

You Have a Gift

I recently held a two-day leadership conference with a particularly receptive audience. Like me, they all had a story. There were a lot of laughs, tears, sighs, shouts of joy, and some real "ah-ha" moments. I realized that my gift had enabled me to lead and inspire a room of important people who also had gifts waiting to be cultivated. If they could identify and nourish those gifts, they could also lead and inspire a room of important people. God gives us our gift and what we do with that gift is our gift back to God.

Pastoral Affinity

The conference experience illustrates how powerful and lasting the impact that one person can have through pastoral affinity. In my case it was my pastor, Rev. Walter R. Bauldrick, Sr. He saw something inside me before I was able to recognize it Myself-he saw my gift. He responded to me based on what he believed I could be not how I appeared to him at the time. This is just one example of his pastoral affinity. Ben A. Gibert, my bishop also credits the application of pastoral affinity for his successful ministry of over four thousand members. Pastoral affinity is the God given ability to authentically connect with one another.

The Power of Intentionality

God is the source but we do the work. Things don't just happen, they must be planned. One cannot accidentally succeed over the long-term. The transformation of the soul is an event that begins a process in which a system of principles is necessary. Pastoral affinity is one principle that helped me overcome many obstacles to enjoy blessings in very important areas.

Stop Guessing

Are you working long, hard hours without the results you were hoping for? Is it possible to develop life skills that will enable you to accomplish your dreams and goals? The answer is yes! It's not only possible, but habitual. First we form our habits and then our habits form us.

The Solution

I teach pastors and their leaders who feel empty, frustrated, and wonder if they've missed their purpose because they aren't seeing enough results. I show them how to discover purpose and move toward it- more easily avoiding the frustration that comes from guessing through their ministry.

Take Action

If left untreated, discouragement can lead to despair, a sense of unfaithfulness leading to loss of hope. Which is one of the main reasons people leave the ministry- they stop growing. If you feel like the stress of running the ministry is keeping you from reaching your full potential, perhaps you'd like some help. I enjoy providing the specific blueprint on how to foster your ministry through pastoral affinity and marketing.

ABOUT THE AUTHOR

James D. Foster, PhD (Dr. James) helps pastors elevate their ministry by directing them to leverage the art and science of pastoral affinity. Implementing these teachings, pastors are empowered to attract more members, effectively solve problems, and turn their gifts and talents into revenue. He is a pastor, theologian, author, teaching veteran, and pastoral marketing expert with a proven track record. An experienced keynote speaker and leadership coach, Dr. James earned his Ph.D. in Theological & Historical Studies from Garrett at Northwestern University. He is Sr. Pastor of Chicago World Outreach. Learn more about him and his services at www.pastoralmarketing.com, www.fosteryourministry.com & www.chicagoworldoutreach.org.

twitter.com/FosterYourLife

www.linkedin.com/profile/view?id=126420471

www.facebook.com/pastorjames.foster

DOING WHAT COMES NATURALLY

by Lee Collins

I was 18 years old when I got my first job. It was at a McDonalds and I worked there for one month. But in a moment I will share with you how that one short month set the direction for my life's work.

The story really began after I left McDonalds. The year was 1988 when I was hired to work at the Winn-Dixie Deli in Camden, South Carolina.

I was still in high school and it was unusual for a student to be given a job working in the deli. We were usually used to fill bag boy or stocking spots. Because of this I felt it was a great privilege to have that job, I was determined to make the most of it, and to date it has probably been one of the most fun jobs in my entire life.

I had been working at the deli for about six months, training on properly handling and cutting meat, baking and decorating cakes, repackaging cheese, making doughnuts, and occasionally helping with inventory, when one afternoon in an unusual break room conversation I identified and brought to my manager's attention seven things we could do to make the deli work better.

He laughed and shooed me away to the front counter to help a customer. I felt completely rejected. But, what seasoned manager would listen to an 18-year old punk kid with grand ideas about how to make HIS deli work better?

About a month later another interesting event took place. Sunday was usually a slow day and because other employees were on vacation there was simply nobody else available. So for the first time ever, the entire deli was left in the hands of an 18-year old high school kid. What could go wrong?

I privately saw this as an opportunity to test my ideas, and I was both excited and nervous. I have always thought "differently" and I knew if my ideas worked, I would show my boss and prove to him they were valid. If they didn't work, as long as I didn't burn the place down, I figured I could just quietly remove everything and nobody would be the wiser.

Sunday was only four days away and I had much to do.

The good news is that nothing bad happened. I spent the day implementing, testing and tweaking my processes all the while happily taking care of customers with their deli meat and cake decorating needs.

But what happened next was one of the scariest moments of my life (at the time anyway).

Have you ever been in school and heard your name on the intercom telling you to come to the principal's office? It was the next morning during homeroom when this happened to me. I immediately broke out in a cold sweat not having any idea why or what I may have done, so I walked to the principal's office, head hung low, preparing to receive whatever was about to happen to me.

It was a phone call from my boss at Winn-Dixie. It was in that moment that I realized I was so busy all day that I forgot to "un-do" all my changes before I went home for the evening. Uh oh.

"Hello?" I said. The voice sternly answered in a booming voice, "Hey Lee, it's Tim, and I want to talk with you about what you did to my deli yesterday."

He continued, "you know you are the first high school student we have EVER let run the deli alone. I have adult employees who have worked here for over two years who I still won't let run the deli alone, but you're in high school and we let you do it after only six months. Then you come to me with these crazy ideas that I clearly told you to NOT do."

In a panic I replied, "I'm sorry, I will come in today on my own time and put it all back the way it was… I really just wanted to try to help."

His voice softened, "Lee, you shouldn't have done this without my permission, but I love what you did. It works and I don't want you to change it back – I want you to help me prepare this to present in the regional manager's meeting next month."

I was thrilled!

What Tim didn't know is while working at McDonalds a spark was ignited inside me. If I and my teenage friends could be trusted to run a multi-million dollar franchise using wall charts and a dishcloth I knew I needed to pay attention. And the opportunity to improve how things worked was all around me – I was like a kid in a candy store!

After school that day we worked on documenting the changes, with Tim adding his well-seasoned spin to them.

Tim knew I had been considering the military, so that afternoon he shared with me that I was being considered for his management position (he was being promoted). I was flattered but kindly refused and left the next month for USAF basic training.

I never heard what happened at the meeting. Not until years later.

In 1996, eight years later, I was visiting my parents and found a "Winn Dixie Handbook" on the coffee table. My mom had taken a part-time job in the deli. Having nothing else to do I flipped through the handbook. Right there in front of me I found the same exact same guidelines and processes I wrote in 1988, and they are still in use today as part of Standard Operating Procedure in all Winn Dixie delis around the country.

I was completely blown away. At eighteen-years old with NO formal business or marketing training, I re-wrote the Winn Dixie Deli standard operating procedures. Since then, my skills have improved.

I spent 9 years in the United States Air Force where I was given the honor of updating and re-writing the training plans for my career field. I became the "trainer's trainer" at a total of three duty stations.

After honorable discharge from the military, I was quickly promoted to Vice President in charge of Network Performance Technology at Bank of America. This small team was later outsourced to EDS and promptly slated to be downsized since it was considered a liability and not a profit center. Instead, during the transition, I took it on myself to guide my small team to re-vamp how we did business and we grew the area from one client to over three hundred multi-million dollar per year clients. This massive growth couldn't be ignored and today, using the same processes I created for getting and keeping clients, they have almost ten-thousand clients.

In 2007, determined that if I can create this kind of success for other people I could surely do it for myself, I left my high-paying corporate role to pursue my own entrepreneurial endeavors, and turned $500 of "seed money" into a prospering six-figure per month business.

The funny thing is I had all but forgotten the story of my humble beginnings at Winn Dixie until I heard a keynote speaker at a marketing event in Denver, Colorado say "the greatest success will come when you enjoy doing what comes naturally to you".

As it turns out I have spent the past twenty-five years doing what comes naturally to me: identifying and resolving business and marketing challenges for myself and other people.

And I'm just getting started...

ABOUT THE AUTHOR

 **Lee Collins** is a direct marketer, copywriter, author, and an in-demand business strategist who believes in thinking differently to solve business challenges. An expert on leveraging systems and processes to enhance profits, Lee has held senior leadership positions in three major US corporations and his unique approach to problem solving has proven effective in twenty-seven different industries. Lee recently helped a company reduce debt by over $700,000 in less than eighteen months, and led another to their first $250,000 month. You can learn more about Lee, his products and services and his creative online and offline strategies for modern business at iStrategery.com and Lee-Collins.com.

www.facebook.com/leecollins

twitter.com/LeeCollins

www.linkedin.com/in/leecollins1

SAIL AWAY GIRL

by M. Elizabeth Aristeguieta

have lust in my heart. Wanderlust that is. For as long as I can remember, I have wanted to sail around the world. When someone asks me how I would spend my money if I won the lottery, amongst some other frivolous things, I have always said that I would go to the Cote D'Azur, purchase a sailboat, and hire a crew of seven Italian sailors. People immediately attribute the third thing to a different kind of lust even though I REALLY am looking for crew. So they're attractive, what's wrong with that?

Besides sailing, I love to cook and feed people. Growing up I thought I wanted to be a pharmacist until I went to college and discovered that there were no beakers and Bunsen burners, just books, books, and more books. I guess I wanted to be a bit of a mad scientist and mix chemicals and light things on fire. As it turns out, cooking is a little bit like mad science behind a stove.

In all my years of traveling, I have always made it a point to learn about the cuisine of the particular region or city that I am visiting. On a trip to Italy with friends, I found out in advance what the specialty was for each city we went to, purchased it, and shared it with everyone on the bus…with wine of course. What struck me was how genuinely thrilled the local vendors were when I came looking for their specialty food; they were always eager to share information about it with me. So while others were buying trinkets, I was feeding my brain (and my belly) with information that will last me forever in the form of a small taste of the area. Little did I know that my mission in life had been percolating inside for years and years.

I am aware that what I want to do is a very romantic and adventurous thing, but I would not want it any other way. I intend to sail to every port possible, meet with the locals, and have them show me how to cook one of their favorite childhood meals and then learn the background behind each meal. I want to marry the history of the meal with the region. Today we have the ability to get food from anywhere at any time and I fear that we will lose some of our cultural ties to where we come from and the why behind the food our ancestors made.

My other connection to travel and food is my father. He loved food and he made us try things as kids that I know I would have never tried if he had actually told us what they were before we ate them. He once told us that rabbit cooked in a paella in an orange grove in Valencia, Spain was chicken and that fried squid (aka calamari) was onion rings. It was only once that we gave him the stamp of approval when he confessed to what we were really eating. I remember him eating baby eels in squid ink all the time and innards of every animal imaginable. He could not trick us into eating those things, try as he might. Sorry, but brains look like brains even when they are cooked! God love my mother, he made her cook all kinds of wild stuff for him. She is a fabulous cook and she cooks food from all over the world except innards and baby eels in squid ink, thank goodness.

One of my favorite childhood memories is of a trip we took that my father had planned completely around restaurants. One day, instead of going to a restaurant, we just pulled over and ate along the side of a road somewhere in France under a tree and next to some cows. My dad had run into a local store and purchased some bread, cheese, and cold cuts along with the wine of the region, and we sat there and ate in the warm afternoon. I still have the wine bottle opener from that day, and I confess that a little wine, bread, cheese, and cold cuts will always be comfort food to me.

On that same trip, we went to several gorgeous wineries, including one in Champagne, and we all got to try a sip at each one. We thought it was a huge deal to be able to drink alcohol, as we were nowhere near the drinking age in the States. I remember how nice all of the people were and how they made sure we learned something during our visit, and I will never forget the rows and rows of Champagne bottles with their bottoms up in the air waiting for their turn with the riddler.

On a vacation I took with my mom after my dad passed, we sailed from Norway to the outer Hebrides Islands. Everywhere we sailed we would spend the first half of the day touring the main sites, and the second half of the day was usually spent at the local pub talking with the people who lived on those tiny islands. We both remember the people more than the sites, although I admit the standing stones we saw were pretty cool.

I have determined that my bond with the sea has been passed down from ancient generations through my DNA. I have always found the sea to be a source of rejuvenation, and I love being on a boat. I think on almost every vacation I have taken as an adult I have either been on a boat for the entire trip or somehow found a boat to see something or relax on, even if it was a simple ferry ride. So it must be in my blood. On a trip to Belize, we were returning from a jungle tour on a boat, and the owner, who had the cleanest boat on earth, asked me if I wanted to take the helm. I think the entire boat gasped in utter shock that this guy would let anyone other than himself at the helm. I was shocked myself and never knew why he selected me out of the ten or so folks on the boat. This has happened to me before, so I must have a subliminal message across my forehead that says "must drive boat."

So now I am Sail Away Girl.

There are many more adventures to foreign lands to come. On my travels I collect recipes and the stories behind them for my upcoming cookbook in hopes of bringing the world a little closer together by sharing what is common to us all…food and family. My next big journey is set to begin in 2015. You can follow along as I make preparations to sail, learn a bit about sailing and cooking in different parts of the world (along with yummy recipes), and cast off with me at www.sailawaygirl.com.

See you on the water,

Sail Away Girl

ABOUT THE AUTHOR

 **Elizabeth Aristeguieta**, aka Sail Away Girl, is an entrepreneur, avid sailor, and cook. Ms. Aristeguieta has started several successful small businesses including a commercial mortgage company, three assisted living facilities, a real estate development company, a website development company, and most recently, a catering company. Ms. Aristeguieta is currently planning to commence a sail around the world in 2015, in which she plans to cook with the locals at every port she visits. Ms. Aristeguieta received a BA in accounting from the University of Texas in San Antonio and has taken numerous culinary instruction courses from various culinary institutes including Le Cordon Bleu and Kendall College in Chicago, Illinois.

To travel along with Elizabeth through her stories at www.sailawaygirl.com.

facebook.com/sailawaygirl

twitter.com/sailawaygirl1

www.linkedin.com/in/elizabetharisteguieta/

WIPING FEAR OFF THE MAP

by Sonya Ramsey

My twin sister Tonya and I grew up in public housing in Detroit, Michigan in the '70s and were bused to Marquette Elementary School. As a kid, I was oblivious to what busing was; I was just a kid who loved to go to school.

Those were good times! On the bus rides to and from school, I'd press my head against the window and dream about what life would be like if I lived in one of the big houses we drove past every day. I became motivated to achieve more in life than what I saw in my environment and decided that an education was the key to success. And then in 1984, my life completely changed.

In June of that year, alone in my room, my heart and mind raced as I reflected on the things my neighbor, Mrs. Holt, had shared with me over the last two years. She loved to talk about how her personal relationship with Jesus Christ had changed her life. Being the curious teen that I was, I would spend hours asking her questions. I wanted to know how her life was different and what it meant to follow the Jesus Christ. "Open your Bible to..." was her common response.

I thought about how she told me that in spite of being a good person, accepting Jesus into your life was true fulfillment (John 10:10). It was at that moment that I prayed and asked Jesus Christ to be my Lord and Savior.

My senior year of high school was when I recognized that I needed Jesus to guide my every aspect of my life. After high school, with the Lord's help, I went off to college and earned my engineering degree. Upon graduation, I was divinely appointed to live in Chicago. It was a divine appointment because, despite receiving lower grades than many of my peers, there I was, job offer in hand during a time when jobs were scarce.

I didn't know why the Lord wanted me in Chicago; I trusted His judgment and headed to the Windy City to start my career as a systems engineer with Motorola. After seven years working as a sales engineer, I began to feel restless. Something was missing. I prayed and felt the Lord calling me to a career in sales. Back then I considered myself shy, but when I was selling, I came out of my shell. I loved sales! I would devour books and tapes from sales trainers like Brian Tracey, Tom Hopkins, and Dale Carnegie. I worked in sales for nine years before I forced myself to face reality. As much as I didn't want to believe it, selling products and services for someone else wasn't the path I was destined to take.

I couldn't ignore my desire to start a business; I knew the Lord had planted that seed in my heart. I wasn't pursuing it, but I couldn't shake the feeling either. I began to pray and act on faith. I realized that my true calling was entrepreneurship and decided to start my own coaching/consulting business. Today, I know that He intended me to go out on my own before I actually did, but I allowed fear to delay my destiny. I was so scared to launch a business that I sat on the idea for several years.

How many times has the fear of the unknown paralyzed you from taking action? I decided to stop standing on the sidelines and do something. My mission is to motivate women to conquer their fears and become successful entrepreneurs. God wants more women to enter the marketplace and with proper training, it's possible to avail of God's promises and run a successful business. But as I've learned, it doesn't come without a fight.

If someone asked me what my clients and potential clients (most of whom are Christian) struggle with in their businesses, the answer, without hesitation, would be allowing fear to hold them back from reaching their full potential. In spite of what the Bible teaches us about fear, we often remain paralyzed and our businesses suffer.

Typically, when learning how to overcome fear, we're encouraged to trust in God. The challenge is that most of us trust passively, feeling no need to go further than the decision to trust. But that kind of trust won't help you get past fear. From God's perspective, in every area of our lives, we are not called to be passive. There's something missing.

Like a five year old girl being dropped off by her mom on the first day of school, there was a nervous pit in my stomach when I thought about launching my business website. Like any person of faith, I prayed, read my Bible, and focused on scriptures that talked about overcoming fear. This approach made me realize that my faith wasn't enough; there's another component that most of us overlook.

I joined Toastmasters years ago because I wanted to become a better speaker. During my third meeting, one of the members asked me if I wanted to give my first speech. "Sure!" I confidently replied. The members had no idea how petrified I was to deliver a simple five-minute speech.

That weekend, I began outlining my speech. The toughest part was picking a topic. I finally settled on the theme, "Life Changing Event," and something magical began to happen as I filled in my outline: The fear waned and my confidence grew. The day of my speech, my confidence far outweighed my fear, and I did a great job! I was so excited. What I've now come to recognize is that having a plan help me create that speech.

The successes I experienced soon became my inspiration. I was more determined to conquer my fears and help my clients defeat their own fears and grow their businesses. In order to move past the fear that has taken root in our minds, by faith, we must map out a very specific plan that gets us to the finish line.

All the teachings I've received in both my walk with Christ and business weren't working to the fullest until I realized the power of mind mapping by goals. I love mind maps! They're diagrams that visually outline information created from a central idea with sub-categories branching off the center. From there, ancillary concepts are developed from the sub-categories. Categories can represent words, ideas, tasks, or other items related to a central key word or idea. Mind maps enable us to develop a plan to accomplish the things we fear.

Mind maps have helped me build my confidence and achieve my personal and entrepreneurial goals. Fear no longer lives in the forefront of my mind and heart because I'm focused on implementation. Mind mapping inspired me to create the Visual Freedom System™ (VFS). This system is designed to help you move past your fears and take your business to the next level and is comprised of five steps:

1. Write down the task you're fearful of accomplishing as the focal point.
2. Create a mind map with three paths:
   - Biblical confessions (spiritual);
   - Benefits of completion (emotional); and
   - Breakdown of subtasks (tactical).
3. Decide which subtasks you can complete and seek help completing the remaining subtasks.
4. Develop realistic timelines.
5. Just do it!

You have the ability to take charge of your business! Stop letting fear become your focal point by mapping out a plan. What we typically do to overcome fear has staying power when we combine our own techniques with mind maps. Mind maps produce systems that give us the confidence to complete tasks we are most fearful of.

I'm all about encouraging people to build amazing businesses for the Kingdom of God!

ABOUT THE AUTHOR

 **Sonya Ramsey** is a business strategist, speaker, and author of the book, <u>The Destiny Deception: Satan is Lying to Women Again And What To Do About It</u>! As a devoted follower of Jesus Christ, she is passionate about helping Christian women overcome their limitations and make a difference in the world through entrepreneurship. Her mission is to empower these women to create and grow businesses that attract high-paying clients AND attain spiritual, physical, and financial prosperity.

Sonya's ability to listen, create solutions, and develop systems that simplify seemingly complicated concepts has motivated her clients to take action and grow their businesses. To learn more about the VFS, send an email to <u>support@TheChristianBusinessCoach.com</u> with "VFS Map" in the subject line or visit <u>www.TheChristianBusinessCoach.com</u>.

facebook.com/TheChristianBusinessCoach

twitter.com/sonya_ramsey

NEVER JUDGE A BOOK BY IT'S COVER

by Reginald Wilson

can picture it as if it were yesterday. The young boy would not look up at me to smile or make eye contact. Could it be that he doesn't understand my language? Is he having a problem hearing me? Or maybe he is dumb and deaf? I again tried to make a connection; however, this time I was friendlier and used my congenial voice, thinking I could at least illicit some sort of eye contact. Nothing ... no response. Surely he must want to ask me something or wonder why I am in his working space. What could cause a person to feel so bad about themselves that they would not even lift up their head to speak when spoken to? Even a dog would wag its tail and a tired old cat would rub up against you when it feels love.

I started to put things into perspective. I was visiting a foreign country and had been instructed not to go outside at night or walk the streets because of the possibility of being taken hostage, kidnapped, or even murdered. It was 1994, and this country was in an uproar. People, even youths, began to stand up and fight for their freedom.

My parents divorced when I was young, and my mother was left to raise three children on her own. I thought back to our struggles and understood the young boy's pain. After nineteen years of surviving by fighting with my hands or outsmarting others, it became apparent that the life I came from was no walk in the park. Actually in my neighborhood we didn't have parks; we played in the streets or in corner vacant lots. In school, our teachers inspired our future careers by posting great big pictures on the wall. Our options were teacher, preacher, fireman, policeman, entertainer, or athlete. These were the limitations imposed on us and we were not to have expectations of grandeur.

Before I fast forward to the present, let me go back to why I was concerned about the young boy who would not look me in the eye. From the day I was born, my life was plagued with challenges. As the years went by, I started taking risks to escape my life of poverty. Soon I indulged in the wrong things, which hurt the people around me and caused them to hurt more people. If you do not believe miracles happen, maybe by the time you finish reading this you will be enlightened. The God who created each of us is waiting for the right time and the right place to show us what little we know.

My misery became the tools of my success. My mother, who trained me as a professional musician, laid a foundation that came out of years of adversity. I was taught not to forget where I came from or the struggles I went through. These lessons contributed to my compassion for helping others. I grew up in a city where I was told: "Don't drink that water, it is not for coloreds!" "Go to the back of the bus where you belong!" "What are you doing in this community?" "People like you don't belong here." "If something is missing you must have stolen it." Because my skin is dark, it was usually assumed that I was doing something wrong. Not having a connection with that young boy was a flashback.

Twenty years later, I have been to twenty-eight countries on five continents. Before traveling the world, I played music in the French Quarter of New Orleans and toured with Clarence Carter, Jean Knight, and James Brown, to name a few. Today I help restore lives, write, speak, and show organizations, such as to governments, businesses communities, and churches, how to uncover the keys to relationships. Many have called me a "Game Changer" or a "Play Maker."

During my journeys as a minister, I found great treasures in the most unlikely places. For instance, in New Orleans I was visiting a business and met a young man from Panama who was the building's parking attendant. Upon returning to receive my car, I asked this young man a challenging question: "Young man, what are going to do with your life? Is your life's ambition to park cars?"

"Oh no," he replied, "I am going to do something great with my life. I want to go to college and study computers and make something of myself. I asked him how he was going to make that happen and he told me he was going to get an education. Then I asked him if I could help him set up an interview at a prestigious college would he be interested. He happily replied, "Count me in." The outcome was awesome. I had just connected with this university a month earlier, and while visiting their campus, I was privileged to sit with the university president. During that visit, I asked him if I were to bring a group of young minorities to campus, would they consider interviewing them for enrollment. It would be a challenge for them to make the necessary adjustments to enroll some of these kids, but he accepted my proposal.

The young man was accepted, even though his ACT test score was below their requirements. The story gets better. Five years later, I received a phone call from the president. Believe it or not, he said, "Pastor, you need to come and see that young man graduate." When it was time for the young man to walk across the platform, the president took the microphone and said, "This young man struggled at the beginning and it has taken him a year longer to graduate, but once his feet got on the ground, he never stopped running. I would like to announce to this audience that Mr. West is the first black man from Panama in the history of our university to graduate. Not only that, but he is coming out as an undergrad with the highest guaranteed salary ever for our university." The applause was astounding as the audience rose to their feet.

So what do I do? I challenge people to give their best by waking up their hidden treasure and bringing it forth. I prove the truth, which Dr. Martin Luther King spoke, that a person should not be judged by the color of his or her skin but by the stature of his or her character. Over and over I've been able to persuade others that failure is not an option—it's only a step toward future success. Like Mr. West discovered, dreaming big and believing in people is sometimes all you need to bring you face-to-face with your designed destiny. I help people discover hope in crisis and find their due purpose and valuable mission in life. I raise up leaders who are sick and tired of falling short in their results. I raise up young people who've never been exposed to the possibilities of God's ability. I build houses, communities, schools, and families through education and forming effective networks that work!

All that I have said is not who I am, it is what I do! Honestly, I am the neighbor next door who you never knew. South Africa, before the fall of Apartheid, could not keep me, the hood could not defeat me, and no one else could prevent me from being proud of my deep black skin. Remember to be mindful of your neighbor, for I am the one next door; that genius you never knew!

ABOUT THE AUTHOR

Dr. Reginald Wilson is an author, entrepreneur, builder, investor, life coach, speaker, television host and an ordained minister who is affectionately known for his humor and optimism. He is the founder of Fulfilling The Gospel Ministries International. Prior to Hurricane Katrina, Dr. Wilson and his wife also founded two schools, Innovative School of Excellence for Children and School of Ministries International College. He desires to spend the rest of his years developing life coaches, strengthening families, and planting schools and churches all over the world.

Dr. Wilson and his wife Vera of 37 years reside in Terrytown, LA. All four of their children are grown professional adults, and their greatest joy is being grandparents of twelve lovely children.

To find out more about Dr. Wilson, visit his website at: www.largemoments.com

facebook.com/Globalh

twitter.com/apostleconnect

www.linkedin.com/pub/reggie-wilson/31/1b7/52b

THE CRUSHER OF LIMITING BELIEFS

by Lorinda Clausen

grew up in a small South Dakota town, population 898, on the rugged prairie of the Missouri River plateau. The nearest McDonald's was 120 miles away and a one-way trip to the orthodontist was a three-hour drive. Rattlesnakes and mountain lions would frequently make their way to the edge of town. Luckily for my safety, my childhood home was one block from Main Street and that, perhaps, is where my love of urban living developed.

When I turned thirteen, I was–according to the unwritten rules of rural South Dakota life–allowed to start driving. Our groovy wood paneled station wagon was unavailable that day and I was left with "Gertrude," the old green pick-up truck that spent most of its life parked in our driveway. My mom rode in the passenger seat, my younger brother and his buddy in the truck bed. The truck was a classic "four on the floor" transmission with a sensitive clutch–a perfect set up for disaster for a teenaged girl with limited driving experience. I screeched and stopped five times, started up again, and eventually peeled out of the driveway, leaving tire marks on the cement and the two young boys battered from being thrown back and forth against the side of the truck bed.

When we returned home, my dad was watching "The Love Boat" and drinking a Mountain Dew, waiting to hear about my adventure. After listening to my brother's disparaging remarks and my mom's words of praise, my dad said something I'll never forget: "Lorinda, if you can drive that truck, you can drive anything." I felt empowered! Like I could drive backwards in rush hour traffic. Like I could steer the car successfully through a maze of fine crystal blindfolded and on fire. Like I could be the first woman President. Like I could do anything! I was born anew that day as the "Crusher of Limiting Beliefs."

My work history illustrates this sense of confidence. At age fourteen, I was supervising eighteen-year-olds at the community youth center. In college, I was working at a group home where I regularly encountered conflict, emotional outbursts, and the occasional air-born coffee table. My first job out of college required me to move to Japan in order to teach English to Japanese high school students. I was the only one in that school who spoke English as a first language. On spring break, I travelled to China by myself, with only a backpack filled with supplies and my Lonely Planet Travel Guide. I did not speak or understand Chinese, I didn't know anyone there, and I failed to inform anyone back home about my whereabouts. I was adventurous, independent, and naively fearless. At any rate, my father's words rang true: "Lorinda, if you can do this, you can do anything."

I eventually returned stateside and earned my Master's in youth work and leadership and spent the next fifteen years at a nonprofit, advising teenagers and their parents, working on capital campaign fundraisers, leading strategic planning sessions, and taking teenagers on service trips all around the world. I vividly remember breaking up a fist fight between two moms, convincing a heartbroken high school boy not to lie down in the middle of a busy street, listening to a young girl proclaim she was a goat-sacrificing Satanist, and being hounded by the organization's accountant for receipts for bread and eggs purchased at a remote Romanian orphanage, all within a thirty minute time frame. "Lorinda, if you can do this, you can do anything."

As years went by, I began to feel restless—somehow threats of goat sacrifices weren't challenging me anymore. With the advice and encouragement of trusted friends, I resigned my post, started a life coaching business, and found myself yawning far too much. I went back to grad school and studied organizational development and business. After rigorous training, I emerged as a certified Business Coach and a certified Master Executive Coach.

I quickly learned that executive leaders manage a mind-bending level of complexity. They're expected to accomplish a myriad of things with minimal resources. They're counted on to cope with epic levels of uncertainty, market volatility, and a historically record-setting rate of change in information management and technology. The success of a company is dependent on their ability to inspire, mobilize, and engage their employees. As executive leaders, they handle all these challenges IN ADDITION to balancing personal relationships, managing stress, keeping their integrity intact, and circumventing burnout. This is exactly the type of leader I love to coach!

Executive Coaching is a challenge that keeps me interested and engages me. My passion runs deep for situations that remind me of my dad's words. My approach is not fluffy, feel-good coaching; I am brutally honest. I challenge, exhort, and hold people accountable. I want my clients to know that together we can crush the limiting beliefs that keep them from living the life they really want. In addition to being tough, I am generous with my focus and attention. I am their biggest fan and greatest supporter. I intuitively recognize when a client's stress level has reached its maximum point of capacity and when it's time to be gentle and soulful. My coaching produces results that an executive dashboard cannot measure: renewed creativity, fresh vision, and fearless inspiration.

I can talk with executives about their sustainable competitive advantage and EBITDA margin. I can discuss their core leadership competencies and set up a plan to maximize their skills. We can wax eloquent on the theory of what drives disruptive innovation and debate about the ratio of balance needed between deliberate strategies and emerging strategies. But because we are all gloriously human, most Executive Coaching engagements inevitably move beyond business strategy and leadership tactics and get straight to the heart of the matter.

It might be work-life balance, concern about a close relationship, or overwhelming stress. Many wonder how to keep their personal integrity intact when profitability seems to require less than stellar human kindness. At this critical juncture, there is one thing that decides the success level of my client: self-awareness. The lack of self-awareness will derail an executive leader's career faster than anything else. Keen self-awareness is the ability to appreciate your perceived positive aspects and potential as well as to accept your negative aspects and limitations and still feel good about yourself. It's a matter of accepting your humanity. How can I say I'm the "Crusher of Limiting Beliefs" and yet say we have limitations? Because believing we don't have limitations is the most limiting belief of all.

As an Executive Coach, I live for the moment my clients begin to completely accept themselves and actually learn to love their own quirkiness and faults. They begin to make adjustments to how they motivate, censure, and empower the staff to crush their limiting beliefs. I'm making a bold statement, but I stand behind it: An executive with business savvy who fully accepts his or her humanity has a massive sustainable financial advantage over the competition.

All my clients have one thing in common: they are successful, resourceful, and intelligent individuals who aren't afraid of the hard stuff. They transcend their limiting beliefs in order to live the life they really want. I'm simply here to remind them: "If you can do that, you can do anything."

ABOUT THE AUTHOR

 **Lorinda Clausen** is an expert at helping executive leaders achieve ambitious performance goals by coaching them to excellence. Her clients call her fearless, brutally honest, empathetic, and insightful. Lorinda also facilitates strategic alignment with executive leadership teams, generating desired results, building strong teams that work for common goals, and implementing ideas to increase revenues and profits. In addition to decades of experience in leadership roles, Lorinda holds a Master's in leadership and has undergone rigorous training with the ICF approved Center for Executive Coaching. She holds a rare double credential as Certified Executive Coach and Master Certified Coach Trainer. Lorinda aspires to continuously learn and is willing to make bold mistakes that lead to progressive change.

To learn more about Lorinda, please visit her website at: www. clausen-consulting.com

facebook.com/lorinda.clausen

twitter.com/iExecutiveCoach

www.linkedin.com/in/lorindaclausen

LIVING FOR THE SPOTLIGHT

by Debra Jason

When I grow up I want to be an actress. At least that's what I thought when I was young.

I loved the spotlight! The attention, the music, the dancing—everything about it. As early as elementary school I wanted to act and so I did. I played Amaryllis in "The Music Man," one of the Von Trapp kids in "The Sound of Music," and sang and danced in "Brigadoon."

As I approached my teen years, I decided I wanted to be a model, another career that would put me in the spotlight. I think I just liked the idea of being the center of attention (or being in front of a camera). I went to the Barbizon School of Modeling; however, things didn't go as I had hoped. After the High School of Performing Arts turned me down and New York modeling agencies said I was too short, I gave up my pre-adolescent dreams.

In college, I started out as a fine arts major because I liked art, but my artistic ability was limited to sketching abstract images (I got an "A" for effort in high school). When one of my next-door neighbors told me about her career in speech pathology, I thought that sounded cool.

I shared my thoughts with my mom, but her first reaction was, "You wouldn't like that."

I ignored my mother's opinion and went on to receive my Bachelor's and Master's in communication disorders. Alas, my mom was right. It took me six years of schooling and two-and-a-half years working as a speech pathologist in the public school system to realize I wasn't happy. I was fortunate to have a boss who saw my dissatisfaction and with his support, I decided it was time to move on.

I also worked as a disco dance instructor and DJ by night. I loved that job. It was fun dancing, spinning records, and being the center of attention (yes, it was back in the day of record albums). Although a really fun job that connected me with fantastic people, spinning records wasn't a full-time career that paid the bills. BUT I had no idea what career path to take next. That's when I read and followed the exercises in <u>What Color is Your Parachute?</u> It really helped me move forward. I eventually found a new career in the wholesale end of the clothing business and the perks were great—I wore the latest fashions and traveled around the country attending trade shows, but to make a long story short, I changed careers again.

It was in the late Eighties that I realized I wanted to write. I had written poetry as a kid and I felt that creative bug biting again, so I decided to become a copywriter.

One catch….

I had no training or experience. I didn't have a journalism or English literature degree, but I did have a job. And, as fate would have it, I had been appointed project manager of a catalog at a local company. We hired copywriters to write the item descriptions and one day I went to my boss and told her (well, maybe I asked first) that I wanted to write the copy. If she liked my work, we'd save money. If not, we'd go back to the copywriters.

Thus began my copywriting career. I wrote about novelty gift items, t-shirts, and out-of-the-ordinary gadgets. However, after twelve years in business, I was sad to say that the catalog company started shrinking. When I was offered a job in New York, I went (I was born and raised there). But after a year-and-a-half and some unkept promises, Colorado's blue skies called me back.

I returned to Boulder during a state recession. When looking for a job, I heard the same thing from every agency I approached: "Sorry, we're not hiring. We're laying people off right now. "I was petrified. How was I going to pay my bills, not to mention my mortgage? Talk about scary. But then it struck me like a lightning bolt.

In addition to being told, "We're laying people off right now," many of the people I interviewed with also told me that although they couldn't hire me as a salaried employee. However, they would be interested in contracting my services on a freelance basis. I took this as a sign from above. It was my opportunity to grab the bull by the horns and start my own business. The Write Direction was born on January 1, 1989.

Now keep in mind, I had no clients. Many freelance copywriters start their businesses after years of working at an agency and building a client base they take with them. But that wasn't me. I had to start from scratch. Again, talk about scary! However, despite the Colorado recession, I was able to break ground, make an impact, find clients, and establish a successful business. I made a concerted effort to continually market myself; I sent out direct mail letters, networked like crazy, and followed up with phone calls. I took it personally when people said "no thanks" and would have second thoughts thinking, "I must be crazy to do this."

I had very little copywriting experience, but I had two things going for me: two mentors and a strong desire to pursue my dream. My mentors' encouragement gave me the confidence to keep following my dream and twenty-five years later, I'm still here. I started my business more than two decades ago and I know what it takes to get a business off the ground: get the word out to prospects, increase your visibility in the marketplace, and keep your customers coming back again and again. There have been ups and downs, but I stayed the course. I didn't give up. As a result, I've had the good fortune of owning a business that allowed me to live in Boulder, Colorado AND on the magnificent Garden Island of Kaua'i, Hawaii. I consider myself lucky to have three places to call home (NY, Boulder, and Kaua'i).

However, recently I've once again found myself asking, "What do I want to be when I grow up?" I love writing, but it can be a lonely job—it's just me, myself, and my computer. So I started to re-evaluate my path, once again seeking my heart's message. I realized that what I value the most is building relationships. For years, my friends have said that I'm the "glue that holds them together." Jokingly, I'd say, "If only I could bottle that and make it a business." Well, I'm going to do it. I'm transforming my business into one that allows me to form communities and lets me live out my childhood dream of being in the spotlight.

While I've delivered many presentations over the years, both on and off-line, my new venture allows me to get on the stage and connect with others, create a community, and provide valuable information that helps them succeed. As a multi-faceted marketing maven, copywriting and connection coach, I'm pulling back the curtain and sharing with other creative solopreneurs and freelancers what's worked for me. I educate and inspire others to create a lifestyle that provides flexibility, fun, and the freedom to do what they love with people who they love working with.

I encourage others to journey down the road to a freedom-based lifestyle business because I believe it's time for each of us to let our lights shine and live our dreams. Don't hold back; others want what YOU have to offer. You can help them transform their lives and you CAN make a difference. I know you can.

ABOUT THE AUTHOR

Debra Jason founded <u>The Write Direction</u> in 1989 and has since been quoted in books on freelancing and direct response copywriting. She has been a featured guest on on-line programs and has presented numerous live workshops on marketing, social media, and copywriting.

A recipient of the "Creative Person of the Year" award, Debra educates and inspires creative solopreneurs, business owners, and freelancers to create a lifestyle business that provides them with the flexibility, fun, and freedom to do what they love. She also inspires her clients to communicate their message in a way that captivates and converts their prospects into loyal customers.

To learn more about Debra, please visit www.WriteDirection.com.

facebook.com/writedirection

twitter.com/mktgcopywriter

linkedin.com/in/debrajason

A TOOL FOR BUSINESS SUCCESS – THE POWER OF STORY

by Gary Rushin

G rowing up in the Bronx equipped me to thrive. Figuring out what to do for the day was life. My friends (who were all two or three years older) and I were interested in girls, partying, and drinking cheap wine before going to a party. Life was about listening to the sounds of James Brown, the Supremes, and the Jackson Five and watching movies such as "They Call Me Mister Tibbs," "Shaft," "Cotton Comes to Harlem," and "Super Fly." We would often take the old 3rd Avenue El subway and smell the Caribbean aroma of a "cuchifritos" Puerto Rican eatery while hearing the salsa sounds of Tito Puente or Eddie Palmieri blasting from a South Bronx apartment building. We held our noses to avoid the pungent smells of urine while walking up the stairwell of a tenement or riding in an elevator in the "projects." This was my world.

Some of my buddies were members of gangs (InterCrime, Black Spades, and Savage Skulls). I did not join out of the fear of disappointing my parents. My parents divorced when I was six, but my father was always there. He took us to every museum in NYC, to the top of the Empire State Building, and we watched the Yankees from the bleachers. Exposure is powerful. Unlike my friends, I knew that there was life outside of the Bronx.

When I was in the 8th grade, hanging out with my friends abruptly ended. My oldest brother surprised me and agreed to let me, his junior high school kid brother, hang out with him in Greenwich Village at New York University. This was my first time in the culturally invigorating Village and my first glimpse at college life, and I knew this was for me. Sporting a "Dr. J" Julius Erving-like big Afro with "peach fuzz" on my chin, I knew I could pass as a college student. From that day on, going to NYU and Columbia U events and hanging out in Manhattan became my weekend ritual, but without my buddies. This was the new Gary.

At five in the morning, Manhattan's nightlife started winding down and getting on a cold, dirty, graffiti laden subway to go home was the norm. Dealing with a smelly panhandler begging for change or a drug induced homeless person taking up an entire subway car seat was expected. To avoid boredom during the hour ride, I would study the faces of the passengers, who were mostly poor. Dried, weathered, and cracked, their expressions looked like death. I told myself I would not end up like that and started thinking about what I was going to do after high school.

Fast-forward to my sophomore year in college. Stella Boyce was the name of the person who totally changed my world. She worked in the human resources department at the 1 Wall Street headquarters of a venerable blue blood commercial bank, now BNY Mellon, and hired me on part-time. Surrounded by graduates of Princeton, Harvard, and Chicago and exposed to the Wall Street Journal and the Economist, my eyes where opened to the capital markets and the "art of the deal." This was the beginning of my professional journey and it has been a wonderful excursion.

So what do I do? In short, I leverage my street and corporate experience to help businesses and entrepreneurs create value and flourish. Through the use of stories, most of which are based on my experiences, I provide executive education to entrepreneurs and professionals in order to help them strive.

I think about the days when I lived in the Bronx, and about the days I lived in the Grant Projects in Harlem. I think about the days I spent as an international commercial lender covering Southeast Asia and the Middle East. I think about the day I got the financing for Rupert Murdock to form the Fox Network. And I think about the day I was wearing a suit in the jungles of Sumatra with Sukanto Tanoto, who built a resource-based manufacturing empire and is now the richest man in Indonesia. Through these stories, I can teach others how to view an acquisition, value the target company, and finance the deal, which is the type of knowledge entrepreneurs want.

Let me tell you about the story of a high school kid and his friend who developed technology in a garage to fund their start-up company. No! This is not the story of Steve Jobs and Steve Wozniak. This is a story about another young driven entrepreneur who bought Sylvan Learning Systems, the training and testing company later to become Laureate Education, Inc., which provides undergraduate, master's, and doctoral programs for students globally. Yes, it was Douglas "Doug" Becker, the CEO who developed his first company as a high school kid.

It is difficult for a start-up to obtain the capital, develop strategy, and gain synergy that they need to thrive. Entrepreneurs and business professionals can gain from the stories of business success as well as stories of business failure. For example, in a white-washed Miami based building, I was sitting in an orange-colored shag carpeted boardroom (circa 1960s) being presented with the orderly liquidation plan of Eastern Airlines, which once stood with other bygone giants such as Pan Am, TWA, and Northwest. I was the lead member of the executive committee. The greatest success lessons I have learned are from business failures. You come to discover that failure teaches you what not to do and how to succeed. Distress forces you to view business from a "different lens," focusing on strategy, best practices, and value creation. You learn that even the best companies can fail.

So when did I first use story as a tool? It was 2007—show time! I entered a classroom of 50 of so executives; armed with a translator, my presentation, and excitement, I engaged the audience Oprah-like, using story to teach these executive level Chinese MBA students. Some of these students were millionaires, "Asian Dragons" released from economic bondage who created unbelievable wealth. Their ferocious thirst for business knowledge empowered me to use story as an effective tool. I knew I needed to create this same value through the use of story, but at home. It is about teaching lessons learned and integrating techniques with story to be effective. I leverage story and social media to create business programs for entrepreneurs and other professionals. Is this the end of my story? I say, "No!"

ABOUT THE AUTHOR

Gary Rushing is a lecturer, writer, and business specialist in the areas of entrepreneurship, finance, accounting, and banking. Gary blogs on GaryRushin.com, develops executive training programs for entrepreneurs and business professionals, and lectures and consults businesses in China, Europe, Asia, and the US.

A Certified Insolvency and Restructuring Advisor (CIRA) and CPA, Gary has over 30 years of experience. He is a Ph.D. (candidate) in Business Administration, has as MSc in Computer Science, and BBA in accounting. Gary designed courses for the American Institute of Certified Public Accountants and is a former investment/commercial banker, CFO, corporate bankruptcy specialist, and financial risk professional.

facebook.com/gary.rushin
twitter.com/GaryRushin
www.linkedin.com/pub/gary-s-rushin-cpa-cira/0/6a9/5b6

"THE SHAWSHANK REDEMPTION" AND PODCASTING

by Ed Hill

I love the "Shawshank Redemption." It is a wonderfully written masterpiece of a movie with a powerful message of hope that has some great analogies to podcasting. And because I also believe, as a line from the movie so eloquently states, that I have to, "Get busy living or get busy dying"

Like Andy Dufresne (played by Tim Robbins) and Red (played by Morgan Freeman), podcasters are also in prison—creative prison. It's time to break them out with a plan that includes hope, freedom, and redemption. But can you do what Andy did? Is it worth it?

"Andy crawled to freedom through five-hundred yards of shit smelling foulness I can't even imagine, or maybe I just don't want too. Five hundred yards... that's the length of five football fields, just shy of half a mile."

I say yes. I say we have to.

As in "The Shawshank Redemption," podcasters need a hammer, a tunnel, and a big poster! We need to diligently dig every day and hope we find a creative escape that our audience so desperately needs. I've escaped quite a few times in my career with plans that would make Andy Dufresne proud, but somehow I always end up back in the joint. I must create and free myself.

I am in the radio business. And as an internet marketer and entertainer, my in life is to break out of our prison every day with a great idea. When I create, I end up in a place I love with a perfectly executed campaign of authentic writing, performance, and passion that energizes the audience, my peers, and myself. When I do that during my radio broadcast, I am redeemed and in paradise.

Andy Dufresne: You know what the Mexicans say about the Pacific? Red: No.

Andy Dufresne: They say it has no memory. That's where I want to live the rest of my life. A warm place with no memory.

But alas, like the Pacific Ocean, the audience loses their memory of our last great thing and we have to re-create. And until we get our creative mojo back, our audience, our peers, and our growth are locked up with us.

What has happened to the big name Internet podcasters has also happened to some big market radio stations. I listened to the podcast of a very well respected and popular Internet giant. It was horrible, inauthentic, and boring, not to mention rambling and self-indulgent. There was zero entertainment value and it did not establish an emotional and personal connection. That guy is already in podcast prison and does not even know it. I can tell that he thinks he is good, but the audience knows otherwise. It just has not caught up with him yet. His influence and opportunity will wane as will his business. I have seen it time and time again in the radio business.

I wasted three hours one afternoon listening to a top 15 station's talent (a well-known and well-respected veteran). In three hours on a Friday that talent had: 1) no callers on the air, 2) no contesting, and

3) no artist info. No happiness. No excitement. Nothing. And he said the same EXACT THING THE SAME EXACT WAY in 90% of his breaks. This was excruciatingly painful and shocking to hear.

Here are the four primary reasons why Internet podcasts are horrible:

Authenticity, Entertainment, and Emotional Connection

Too many Internet podcaster's have little to no broadcast training. They do not know how to develop and convey authentic personality and emotion nor do they know what entertaining content is. Most of the podcast's I have heard are extremely weak…I mean terrible. Terrible voices. Terrible writing. Terrible music or no music at all and terrible editing with little or no production value.

To succeed in the Internet podcasting world you need to fight and scream for attention. You have to be smarter, cooler, humorous, and more entertaining than anyone else. You need structure, colorful writing, and a funny and emotional connection with the audience. It cannot all be about information; podcasting is broadcasting, a medium of entertainment, information, and emotional connection. You have to deliver all of this and more. The day is here. There are already podcasters who are receiving training and hiring writers and producers. They understand that this will attract a larger audience and influence to their platforms.

The Authentic Personal Stamp

Too many Internet podcasters are either afraid or unable to put their authentic personal stamp on their podcast. The guy selling caramels sounds just like the guy selling a $30,000 sales event. Your podcast has to reflect you.

My radio stations are just like me: loud, aggressive, fun, stupid, cheesy, and fearless; cluttered, crazy, and kind; big hearted, emotional, and competitive; vibrant, alive, and real. If you are afraid to express yourself then your podcast has nothing to say and that is what your listeners will perceive: NOTHING.

Take this "personal stamp" a fellow inmate left on Red:

Red: [narrating] Tommy Williams came to Shawshank in 1965 on a two-year stretch for B&E. That's breaking and entering to you. Young punk. Mr. "Rock and Roll." Cocky as hell. We liked him immediately.

Passionate Connection to Music

Morgan Freeman's character says it best:

Red: I have no idea to this day what those two Italian ladies were singing about. Truth is, I don't want to know. Some things are best left unsaid. I'd like to think they were singing about something so beautiful it can't be expressed in words, and makes your heart ache because of it.

Like Red you must be moved by music and incorporate that emotion into the podcast you are creating. You must use the emotional connection of music to reach your audience!

Too Many Scientists, Not Enough Creationists

This is the most dangerous creative prison to be stuck in. It's a self-imposed maximum-security prison of numbers and averages. Too many times when discussing podcasting, I've heard about branding, strategy, and research but not enough about creativity, writing, and emotion. EMOTIONAL CONNECTION AND AUTHENTICITY ARE WHAT AFFECT YOUR AUDIENCE THE MOST. You must be emotionally authentic.

This is a desperate treatise on podcasters. But I, like Andy, have hope. Hope is what we deliver. Hope is what keeps our audience, our customers, our potential customers, and ourselves motivated and alive.

Andy Dufresne: Remember Red, hope is a good thing, and maybe the best of things, and no good thing ever dies.

Always stay excited about your podcast and deliver that excitement every time.

Red: I find I'm so excited; I can barely sit still or hold a thought in my head. I think it's the excitement only a free man can feel, a free man at the start of a long journey whose conclusion is uncertain.

And, "get busy living or get busy dying." Damn straight advice from a creative broadcasting straight shooter.

I'm in prison now but I'm planning another escape. I've got a hammer, a tunnel, and a big poster and I'm ready to crawl through the hole again.

See you on the other side.

ABOUT THE AUTHOR

Ed Hill is a 25-year broadcast radio veteran and a programming executive with CBS radio. He is a broadcast consultant, media company owner, and a talent coach/consultant. Amonsgt Ed's other skills and accomplishments are movie producer who has worked with an Academy Award-winning director, a music consultant with the NFL, NBS and MLB, and Corporate Creative Director for Citadel/ABC broadcasting. Ed's lesser known accomplishments are worthy of mention as well. He has created a dancing routine with a chicken, held Paris Hilton's hand for sixty seconds, sat next to Roger Ebert at a movie, and composed a country music song with a hit songwriter. Want to learn more about Ed? Visit his website at podstars.net

QUIT TELLING
YOURSELF LINES

by Jason Nicholas

O nce upon a time in a land far, far away there was a handsome prince and...STOP! This is not a fairy tale (although I did end up marrying the princess of my dreams). This story is about an average boy who learned how to embrace the greatest gift of all: imagination.

I did not grow up to be the President, a Nobel Prize winning astrophysicist, an Academy Award winning actor, or a top secret agent (which is a good thing because if I was, I would be out of a job for exposing my identity). I'm just the guy next door—an average Joe (well, Jason) with a family, career, and life of over-commitment. I am a husband, father, architect, artist, improv actor, volunteer, etc. Can you relate?

Life can be overwhelming considering all the different roles we play, not to mention the large amount of external forces, like news and social media, but it's how we operate within these roles and how we use those forces that matters. Over the years I have learned to view my roles as filters of perception for daily invigoration and inspiration. I believe that our imaginations are our most precious gift and my passion is to embrace my imagination to inspire and motivate others.

I express my imagination through the lines in my architectural designs, artwork, the stories I create, and those I deliver in my improv acting. (Do you see a theme here?) I have learned to take all the mishmash in my head from the overload of daily life and channel it into the act of creation. Expressing these tangled thoughts on the canvas of life has enabled me to paint the life I dream of.

Drawing for Connection—
Putting Your Pencil Where Your Mouth Is

When I was seven, I was in a serious accident and hospitalized for weeks. When I returned to school, I wasn't allowed to participate in gym class or go outside at recess and run around and play with my friends. I felt alone in the lunchroom of life, and we all know how awkward it feels to eat alone. To pass time, I drew pictures of cars, houses, and super-heroes, creating my own world on paper. After recess, I would show my friends my drawings and they liked them. I had discovered a way to connect with them on a new level and draw them into my world. This new bond ended the isolation I felt from my separation from the playground.

As kids, we never thought twice about picking up a pencil, marker, or crayon. We weren't worried about our drawings looking realistic—

we doodled for fun. As we grow older, we tend to lose that beautiful childlike freedom of expression and worry about what others will think of us. For me, drawing isn't about being photorealistic, it's about capturing a feeling of time and space; as away of embracing the moment. It's an ultimate expression of ME. Who knew that a mere scribble or an "inkling," as I call it, could be so simple yet so powerful?

For example, recently I took my seven-year-old son out to dinner to celebrate his good grades. I wanted to spend some uninterrupted quality time connecting with him. Sadly, as is becoming the case everywhere we go, there were TVs all over the restaurant. And of course (and you know this if you have children), the TV is like a glowing magnet to my son.

I needed a way to capture his attention. I flipped over the placemat and reached into my pocket. This was going to be a showdown between myself and the local news channel! I pulled out my pen and drew a planetary scene. I asked Noah to add something to this imaginary planet. Before I knew it, Noah was drawing and creating with me. We bonded over aliens and spaceships. So take that television! Chalk one up for the Dadster!

I owe gratitude to my mother for showing me how to connect with people through artwork. When I was young, she painted scenes of barns and flowers on small pieces of slate and made a gift of them. People loved them. The smiles on the recipients' faces were the warmest of heartfelt glows I had ever seen. She was able to bond and transform people's emotions through her creations. It was magical! I've been able to apply this level of bonding to create unique and captivating brands for businesses.

Architecture: "Simplicity is the ultimate sophistication."
—Leonardo da Vinci

Here's the story of a lovely lady… well an average looking man in my case. Ironically, it was Mike Brady from the "Brady Bunch" who sparked my interest in architecture. He worked from home drawing pictures of houses while hanging with his family. It seemed like a dream come true! In addition to Mr. Brady, my father influenced my architectural aspirations. He owned a construction business and I would spend time with him on job sites, watching him utilize his carpentry talents while I schlepped wood around. This first-hand view of the construction industry, as well as an unexplainable addiction to Bob Vila's "This Old House" series, left a permanent blueprint on my mind. So from an early age I wanted to pursue architecture. I graduated in 1994 from the University of Miami with a Bachelor's in architecture and started my own firm in 2003.

For me, architecture is the ultimate harmonious expression of the left and right brain. It is about listening and understanding clients while transforming conceptual ideas into beautiful simple line drawings of structures and spaces that will be erected.

Improv: Drawing Lines of Dialogue from External Input

Improv performing (i.e., "Whose Line Is It Anyway") is one of my joys in life. There is nothing more therapeutic than getting on a stage with my friends and letting free-flow lines of dialogue come out. The scenes performed are not scripted but based on suggestions from the audience and performed on the fly. Applied to the business world, improv exercises are great for team-building and brainstorming, seminars which I offer.

Drawing: A Conclusion

One of the most precious gifts we possess is our imagination, and for me, drawing is one of the most effective ways to express that gift. People have changed the world by showing us what's in their minds. Jim Henson created the "Muppets" from scribbles he kept in his journal. Dr. Seuss wrote and illustrated forty-four children's books. Now it's my turn.

I want to use the gift of my imagination and my passion for drawing to inspire others to dig deep into their inkwell of creativity and express their authentic selves. I believe that everyone has some talent or passion that makes them unique. If I can help others draw out that passion and use it to improve their lives or businesses, then I will have connected the dots on a page in the sketch book of life. Ultimately, my goal is to inspire "aha" moments in life one line at a time.

ABOUT THE AUTHOR

 Born with a pencil in his mouth in 1970, **Jason J. Nicholas** has always been passionate about exploring his creativity (don't worry, the pencil wasn't sharpened). From his childhood architectural dreams to his heart-warming artwork and humor, Jason expresses his inner creativity by sharing the gift of his imagination. Some say he is a combination of Mike Brady and Bob Ross with a touch of Dr. Seuss (without the six kids, cool afro, or Wocket in his pocket). Jason inspires "aha" moments one line at a time through his drawings and stories.

Jason started his architectural firm, j2n Architecture, in 2003 where he expresses his design talent in both commercial and residential projects. He recently launched www.jasonjnicholas.com where he shares his inkling sketches, imagination, wisdom and wit for both individual inspiration and business branding.

facebook.com/J2Nsketch

twitter.com/jasonjnicholas

www.linkedin.com/in/j2narchitecture

SHINING THE LIGHT OF WISDOM

by Debz Collins

have always loved seeing the world though glass. No, not spectacles or a window ... a camera lens. I was fifteen when I bought my first SLR camera with interchangeable lenses and I was in heaven. I would buy first row center court tickets to the Leggs Women's Tennis Tournament in Lakeway, Texas and spend all day taking photos of well-known champions, such as Billie Jean King and Virginia Wade, as well as up-and-comers Chris Evert and Martina Navratilova.

Like many amateur enthusiasts, I thought of photography as a hobby—I never dreamed that I would make a living doing what I loved. I pursued my interest in technology, got a degree in electrical engineering, and went to work for IBM designing disk drives.

My cameras were never far from my side. After I left the corporate world to start my own business, I worked with mentors who honed my skills in photography, graphic design, audio, video, and editing, knowing that these talents would serve me well in my new ventures. And then one day the world changed. The era of digital photography and video exploded the moment reasonably priced personal computer-based editing systems hit the market. I knew in my heart that this was the right time to pursue what I really loved and plunged head first into a video production business. After two years of producing marketing and employee training videos for corporations, I was invited to work with a small production team and travel the world with a well-known peak performance expert. For over fifteen years I have been blessed to be able to weave my many interests (human psychology and performance, computers, photography, video and travel) into a business that helps others pursue their career and business dreams.

The majority of those years were spent focusing on the technical aspects of video production: framing the shot, tweaking the audio, and most importantly, getting the lighting just right. Eventually, I began to look beyond the technical side and discover the secret behind why some videos had a much greater impact than others. That's when it hit me—it is all about the light.

While the light that is directed ON the subject is essential to what we see, the truly powerful element is the light coming OUT of the video. In other words, is the video just a flat recitation of information, (or worse a blathering stream of narcissistic commercialism), or does it truly emit the compelling light of wisdom? Sound too esoteric? Too elusive? Too weird? Let's look for evidence; let's test this woo-woo pixie dust theory for factual support.

I believe that when the ideas and inspiration you impart in the content of your video grab the attention of the targeted person or audience you want to reach, either by seduction or attraction, (and aren't they really the same?), those ideas insert themselves into the conversation taking place in the viewers' conscious and subconscious minds and change their perspective, awareness, and understanding. The evidence, the proof, is measured in the one great observable metric—your audience actually does the thing you want them to do. Your message therefore becomes functional, purposeful, and effectively executes what I call Wisdomography®.

Video has become a must for online marketing and product delivery strategies. It commands a much higher perceived value than text and audio. Through the Internet, we can use videos to connect with multiple senses and employ timing and movement strategies to extend that elusive short attention span we all suffer from. Wisdomography® was born out of my passion for helping experts share their wisdom and get "scene" through the barrage of boring, me-too informational videos distributed all over the web. While working with personal growth, health, and business experts and speakers, I've found that what brings me the most delight and professional satisfaction is drawing out their wisdom and creating videos that effectively communicate that wisdom to their specific audience. It is time to move beyond the Information Age and demand the Wisdom Age.

Most experts who seek my video training or production services recite the exact same information or how-to knowledge that can be found on the Internet (often for free), relying solely on their personality to act as the differentiator. Even if they up their technical game, sharing me-too content is not worth the cloud memory it's stored on. I can create a great looking and sounding video for any client, so it is a waste of my time and theirs if the content does not match or exceed the technical quality of the video.

We've all heard the saying, "Jack of all trades, master of none." This applies to knowledge as well. It's the specialist in any field who is valued and paid the most. If you have a blocked artery and are in danger of suffering from a heart attack, wouldn't you go to a cardiologist or even a general practitioner for treatment?

A great example of spreading wisdom vs. information through video is found on Ted Talks. Given that all Ted videos are professionally produced, the distinguishing factor of the most popular "Talks" on Ted.com in any category are those that shine the light of wisdom; the wisdom that comes from asking probing questions about what you know to be true; the wisdom that pours out when you dare to ask "what if" and question the accepted knowledge base.

If you want to create a message that goes viral, unless you have a cute talking dog or piano playing cat, the best way to get it out there is to create that "ah-ha" moment for your audience and deliver it in a succinct, clear, and captivating video. Deliver that bit of wisdom that has the potential to change the way we work, play, live, parent, accumulate wealth, become healthy, contribute, or celebrate.

An excellent way to craft your message and monetize your expertise is through our Wisdomography® workshop. Using a proven system, the Wisdom Thesis™, in an immersive mastermind experience, we draw out your unique wisdom-level solution for a specific audience that values and is willing to pay for your answer to their problem.

Once your unique solution is identified, we systematically show you how to share your wisdom and find the appropriate medium for you and your message, whether through books, video, or speaking engagements. We provide you with the training, templates, systems, and resources to produce professional quality videos, podcasts, and books. As a bonus, you will walk away with your first wisdom-level video at the end of the workshop.

If you are ready to build a business that you can take pride in by passing on a legacy of wisdom through online videos that create a massive impact, take the first step at Wisdomography.com. If you have something meaningful to say and say it well, commit to incorporating wisdom-level quality in your content, presentation, and technical production and you will outshine your competition and get "scene" in your best light.

Make influential videos that matter!

ABOUT THE AUTHOR

Debz Collins is an author, a speaker, admitted tech geek, and experienced businesswoman. She holds US and International patents in digital learning methodologies and has created companies in the learning/training and marketing sectors, including a 15+ year adventure in professional video production, working behind the scenes with Tony Robbins, Mark Victor Hansen, Keith Cunningham, Ray Edwards, and many more. Debz thrives on creativity, innovation, worldwide adventures, and working with people who have the desire to change the world. Learn her secrets and receive a special gift at www.Wisdomography.com/swdyd.

www.facebook.com/debz.co

www.linkedin.com/profile/view?id=12646160

DISCOVER YOUR OWN INTERNAL NAVIGATION SYSTEM

by Julianne Gardner

Mary had reached a critical turning point or crossroads in her life. She had been praying to God, asking for His guidance about where she should reside and what she should be doing. As she prayed she heard, "Alaska." So she prayed and prayed and then prayed some more. All she heard was, "Alaska." Months went by and Mary began to get frustrated. She felt as if God was not guiding her in her sincere request for direction. One day she decided to go up into the mountains where she would not be distracted but all she kept hearing was, "Alaska, Alaska, Alaska." No matter how many times she heard, "Alaska," she was convinced that there was no way she was going and that this had to be a huge mistake! Suddenly, a little old man appeared on the trail and sat down beside her to rest. He began to tell her a story about Alaska of all things! She could not believe her ears, but finally she got the message—she knew God wanted her to go to Alaska. The very next day Mary booked a flight. Within three days of her arrival she met the man of her dreams and twenty-five years later they are still together, with four grown children, and more in love now than they were when they first met.

Oftentimes when we come to critical turning points or a crossroads in our lives, we don't know which way to turn or if we should turn at all. How do we know the best choice to make in these moments? I believe the answer is found in knowing and understanding the voice of God. Through that understanding we allow Him to become our very own navigation system.

Do you ever get the feeling that God is trying to tell you something? Are you listening? If not, maybe it's because what you are hearing isn't in line with your desires, or maybe it's because you aren't sure that what you are sensing (hearing) is real. Well, it is real and I believe each of us inherently has the ability to recognize and understand that voice when it tells us what direction to take and the best decisions to make. I also believe that whether we are aware of it or not, each of us, at one time or another, has heard that voice within.

Have you or someone you know ever been "directed" to take a different route home from work or not get on a plane? I think we have all heard stories like this. One that is near and dear to all Americans has been told by those individuals who worked at the Twin Towers and, for whatever reason, chose not go to work on 9/11. These people might have called it intuition or a sixth sense, but whatever it was, they "knew" they shouldn't go to work that day.

Why do we need a navigator in our lives? Well, like the navigation system in our car, which knows how far we need to go, how long it will take us to get there, and what direction we must travel, God acts as a guide by plotting our course and helping us get where we need to go.

Learning to differentiate between the voice of God and that of others takes time. It's one thing to pray and ask for things, it's entirely different to sit, be still, and wait for answers. This takes active listening skills, something that most of us are not taught. The voices we hear may not necessarily be the voice of God, which more times than not, is that still sweet voice inside that nudges us oh so gently.

So how do we develop that ability? There are several practices I have developed over the years that have helped me distinguish between my voice, the voices of others roaming around in my mind, the voice of my ego, and the voice of God. Below, I share three of these and with diligent practice, over time you too will develop the ability to listen more clearly.

1. Introspection: A reflective self-examination and consideration of one's own ideas, thoughts, and feelings. See the "Taking Action" Exercises below.

2. Quiet Contemplation: The state of being silent in order to spend time considering a particular thing in a serious and quiet way. See the "Taking Action" Exercises below.

3. Meditation: A mental discipline in which a person attempts to get beyond the automatic "thinking" mind and develop a deeper relationship with that still small voice inside. To receive a FREE copy of my guided meditation, go to my website and opt in. www.ButterflyEffectMovement.com

Below are what I call "Taking Action" Exercises. Please take some time to consider the following questions:

When challenges arise, whose voices do you hear and what are they saying?

- Parent's voice

  _____

- Society's voice

  _____

- Culture's voice

  _____

- Religion's voice

  _____

Do you know the difference between your own voice and that of others? If you do, specifically explain how you know.

_____

_____

_____

_____

Do you know your voice vs. the voice of God?

_____

_____

_____

_____

What is God telling you to do today?

_____

_____

_____

_____

Let's now examine the negative mind patterns that may be preventing us from listening to our own internal navigation system.

What negative mind patterns are currently directing or guiding your life (i.e., I am no good, I will never amount to anything)?

_____

_____

_____

_____

What have people told you in the past that may be preventing you from Discovering Your True Self, Changing Your Circumstances, and Living a Life of Purpose?

_____

_____

_____

Statistics show that over 65,000 thoughts go through our minds every day and that we make 1,000 decisions based on those thoughts. What do you think is happening to the thoughts we don't act upon? Would you agree that it would be advantageous to become aware of and separate ourselves from our thoughts by identifying them and putting them into perspective and/or releasing them? One of the ways to do this is to become aware of them as they arise and then use that awareness to divert the energy in a positive way.

Some of the more productive ways to divert that energy is to:

- Go for a bike ride, jog, or power walk.
- Stop dead in your tracks and give me twenty push-ups and
- Fifty jumping jacks.
- Use a pattern interrupt method: Clap your hands loudly and say stop.
- Replace the negative thought or belief with one that genuinely supports what you are trying to achieve in your life.

"Finally, brethren, whatsoever things are true, whatsoever things are honest, whatsoever things are just, whatsoever things are pure, whatsoever things are lovely, whatsoever things are of good report; if there be any virtue, and if there be any praise, think on these things" Philippians 4:8 (King James Version).

I am passionate about inspiring people all around the world to transform their lives. I do that through speaking engagements, training workshops, life coaching, spiritual retreats, and through my top selling book, The Butterfly Effect: A Woman's Guide to Discovering Your True Self, Changing Your Circumstances & Living Your Life Purpose.

ABOUT THE AUTHOR

Julianne Gardner is the founder of www.ButterflyEffectMovement. com. She is an international speaker, trainer, coach, and the author of eight inspirational and life changing products including home

study courses, CD's, and her top selling book, The Butterfly Effect: A Woman's Guide to Discovering Your True Self, Changing Your Circumstances & Living Your Life Purpose. Julianne has specialized knowledge in her field of "Transformational Coaching" and provides the highest level of service in her profession. Julianne's energy and passion for life is contagious—she inspires people to follow their true calling and live life to the fullest!

facebook.com/ButterflyEffectMovementInc/

twitter.com/TheButterflyEM

www.linkedin.com/in/butterflyeffectmovement/

STEP AHEAD TO SUCCESS

by A.J. Slivinski

A Drive to Succeed

I learned drive and discipline from my father. He was a physical education teacher and taught my sister and I how to play a variety of sports. During our lessons, we learned to focus on achieving bigger and better results. My father instilled in me a drive that I've carried my whole life and defines who I am. To this day, I have a constant burning desire to achieve, or maybe it's the opposite, maybe it's an extreme fear of failure that keeps me motivated, engaged, and moving forward.

I was taught that if you worked hard, you'd succeed. I worked hard at my business career and reached senior levels of management. It didn't take long for me to realize that climbing the corporate ladder comes with a generous salary and great perks, but there's a catch: I was working sixteen hour days, often seven days a week.

The Two Moments That Changed Our Lives

My wife and I experienced our first watershed moment during the 2000-2001 tech crash. We had invested the majority of our savings in mutual funds and built a diverse portfolio. Then the tech crash came, and we lost 50% of our assets. It became clear that we were not in control of our destiny.

The second watershed moment occurred when I realized I had no control over how I spent my own time. We were on holiday in Europe and instead of relaxing and enjoying time with my wife, I was constantly pulled away from our vacation by the phone.

We finally said, "This has to change." It was a turning point that changed our life.

Together, we committed to getting our time back, while maintaining or improving our standard of living. We investigated how affluent people are able to spend more time at home and still generate an executive-level income. Achieving this status became our primary goal.

I read that 90% of the wealthiest people made their fortune in real estate. We decided to do the same. We sat down in 2002 and devised a five-year plan.

The plan had three components:

1. What we needed to survive.
2. What we needed to be comfortable.
3. What we needed to live lavishly and sustain our current lifestyle.

We meticulously calculated how many condos and apartment buildings we would need to purchase and how much cash flow each one had to produce. Within five years we achieved our goals. I retired from corporate life in 2007 at age 45.

Getting into the "Red Hotel" Business

We started off buying condos, then decided to take the next step. I've always had a desire to learn from the best and to avoid the "trial and error" method when possible. So we acquired a partner and formed a joint venture. This arrangement gave us the confidence to get into what we call the "red hotel" business: apartment buildings. The "red hotel" business is a reference to the number one principle in the game of Monopoly: "Four green houses equals one red hotel." We put up the money and our partner ran the business.

It wasn't long before we learned what our JV partner knew (or rather didn't know) about building a real estate investment business. We believed we could do better. We bought out our partner and we were off and running.

The Current State of Real Estate

Real estate is not exactly a "get rich quick" scheme. It definitely produces a tremendous amount of wealth, but it doesn't happen overnight.

We're not involved in flipping, gambling, or speculating. We study and we do the research. With this approach, we were able to ride out the 2008 crash. We're now in the process of launching a very sophisticated back-end tracking and communication system for our tenants. We can track them from the first phone call to the day they move in. We follow up with information about their status in our loyalty program, upcoming lease renewals, and other issues of concern. We don't just provide information—we listen to our tenants and build communities.

This is the "new economy" in action. Five or ten years ago we couldn't have developed these relationships. Today we possess the know-how and can easily achieve our goals.

We're very optimistic and we have a plan for the next 25 years: build a billion-dollar company. We're building a North American-wide real estate business that merges our roles of real estate investors and property managers.

Essential Lessons for Success

First and foremost, all our success is founded and is the fruit of the love and grace of Jesus Christ. Without the proper foundation, the entire building crumbles. Jesus is the foundation on which we build our lives.

The key to our business success is what we call the "STEP Ahead Success Formula." It's an acronym for our philosophy of business success.

The **S** stands for having a Strategic Vision. My wife and I take this very, very seriously. We periodically leave the house, book a meeting room (complete with flip charts), and conduct a very corporate-like strategic planning session. This process leads us to create, modify, or update our vision while documenting our work product for future use.

The **T** stands for Take Action. You may have a compelling vision and all the plans in the world, but if you don't get out of your chair and actually take action, you won't accomplish anything.

The **E** is for Evaluate. We evaluate our success every quarter. We examine whether we're executing our plans and meeting our targets. We make adjustments and fine tune things and keep moving on. At the end of each year we may tweak the plan again.

Finally, the **P** is all about People. Relationships. If you really want to be successful, you need support—you can't do it alone. If you want to follow an aggressive path, if you want to break the cycle of stagnation, you need to have relationships with people. There's so much to learn from people who are in different fields. And they can help you get to where you want to be, whether through mentoring or by outsourcing some of the work.

What to Do Next

I occasionally get the following question: "AJ, what should I do next if I really want to succeed?"

First, you should evaluate your life. If you're not willing to change or if you're happy with where you are, then you should do nothing.

If change is what you desire, then you need to clearly articulate what that change is. With that in mind, a detailed plan is a must in order to get it done. If you don't have a clear vision, you'll just continue to meander through life.

Most people already know what to do…the challenge lies in getting motivated to take action on that knowledge.

ABOUT THE AUTHOR

AJ Slivinski retired from a successful corporate career at age 45 to become a real estate investor. In six short years, he and his wife grew their investment company exponentially. His portfolio is worth over 22 million dollars and he generated nearly two million in revenues. AJ and his wife began their business in Alberta, Canada and now have a second home in Panama, where they continue to build upon their success. You may contact AJ through his investor website at www.stepaheadinvest.com or email him at aj@stepaheadinvest.com. He looks forward to hearing from you and is eager to answer any questions that you may have.

www.facebook.com/profile.php?id=100002385200297

www.linkedin.com/profile/view?id=21046722

THE MAKING OF A REAL ESTATE POWERHOUSE

by Beth Ryan

I got into real estate as a result of what my family experienced when I was a child. I was the youngest of three and already knew the difficulties families face in affording and realizing their homeownership dreams. The obstacles to purchasing real estate were substantial. A major turning point for me occurred when my family was personally discriminated against in their efforts to purchase a home. From that day forward, my young life's mission was to own a home that I would live in for the rest of my life.

I was brought from Illinois Masonic Hospital in 1961 to a spacious four room apartment. Somehow, my siblings and I, aged one year apart, shared a bedroom on the third floor of a Victorian walk-up, while my parents slept on a pull out couch in the dining room. Within a few years we finally upgraded to a large six room apartment on the second floor of a three story walk up where only the owners were permitted to use the backyard—renters were forced to congregate on the sidewalk and in the street. Life was grand for a few years, then in 1967 the owners of the building decided to sell. We had three months to find a new home.

What sunk in was that we had no say in that decision because we were only renters. This was another turning point in my life. My mother made the prudent decision not to follow the flight to the suburbs and borrow $2,000 from her father to purchase a house. The choice she made was for us to stay in the inner city and attend public schools with the diversification of every ethnicity and amenity that a city has to offer.

I fondly remember the five of us looking at house after house in various neighborhoods with no assistance from a realtor. We finally chose a fixer-upper in a working class neighborhood in Rogers Park. At that time there was no buyer brokerage, thus we were not provided with information about the neighborhood or local school system or what options were available to us such as purchasing the building that we were still living in. At that time, buildings were sold to friends and business partners, not to the tenants who loved them. We later found out that we could have afforded to purchase the building—what a crock! At that moment, I made a silent commitment to myself that I would never ever be put in this type of situation again. I was emboldened to establish a life in which I determined where I lived and had the knowledge and resources to make it happen. As a result of my family's imposed relocation, making this dream a reality for myself as well as for others became my life's mission.

In 1983 I graduated with a finance degree and landed my dream job at a bank in downtown Chicago. Interestingly, I chose location over ownership and stayed in the city. My first apartment was in the Lakeview neighborhood, which is a block from Lake Michigan. At the time, my bank was offering a discount on interest rates to encourage homeownership with no points. Of course I jumped at the opportunity to buy a brand new townhome in my neighborhood. I felt like a kid with a myriad of choices: I was allowed to select colors for the kitchen cabinets, the ceramic tile in the two bathrooms, and the stain on the hardwood floors. Within a year my bank closed and my dream job turned into the unemployment line.

This unfortunate situation brought out the rebel in me. I contemplated over what path to take and decided to become a realtor. I had taken the real estate class in 1981 and with a newly completed MBA paid by the bank, I decided to explore the possibility of becoming a 100 percent commissioned sales agent. The thought of a career in real estate brought up memories of my past and with my business acumen, finance knowledge, and desire to help people, I knew I could be successful in this next phase of my life. I loved the whole process of buying and selling homes, and being able to help the masses while making money was the icing on the cake. Remember, my life's mission was to provide the opportunity for anyone who wanted and had the financial means to purchase a home that they liked, not settle for less than what they wanted.

I was offered a desk job at a real estate office and quickly became a licensed agent. I was subsequently hired at a family owned office in Lincoln Park, Chicago. It took me six months of walking door to door, making calls, and asking everyone I knew to buy or sell. After I sold my first property I was hooked. This experience reinforced my desire to help people purchase properties and provided me with a great income at the same time. After 15 years I opened my own company, Ryan Realty & Associates, Inc. and am now celebrating 25 years of selling real estate and securing my clients' financial success over generations. To make this possible, I have a powerful and resourceful team of bankers, attorneys, estate planners, and accountants who assist with the buying and selling process. My team ensures that my clients attain great success by facilitating some of the largest financial decisions of their lives.

I want to end this article by sharing an experience that shocked the living daylights out of me. I had been working with a client for over twenty years, helping him upgrade his home purchases and make investments. One day he called and announced that he wanted to upgrade to an elegant multi-unit property. Here's the interesting part: He wanted to buy it sight unseen, based solely on my recommendation. He told me that he had complete confidence in me and that if I thought it was a good investment then it was. This experience made me reflect on the many clients I have worked with in the US as well as internationally who continue to place their trust in me. They know that I always do right by them and have their best interests at heart.

Interestingly, I have never focused on the money but on delivering quality service to my clients and meeting their needs in a timely and compassionate manner. With that as my focus, I know the money will come, and it continues to flow. I truly believe that when you give to the world, it gives back to you tenfold. Dream big; make it real and tangible. Do what it takes to live that dream each and every day. Live a life filled with bountiful blessings and a win-win attitude.

ABOUT THE AUTHOR

Beth Ryan is a negotiating powerhouse, steering her clients' real estate success at the helm of her firm, Ryan Realty & Associates Inc. Beth and her award winning team work closely with US and international clients to build solid real estate investment strategies that will support short and long- term life goals. Beth attributes her continued success to the strong business and financial acumen she brings to each engagement and the depth of her knowledge of neighborhoods, properties, and the real estate market. If you would like to learn more about what this successful woman and her team can do for you, visit her website, www.RyanRealtyChicago.com.

www.facebook.com/pages/Ryan-Realty-Associates-in-Chicago/138152102885331

twitter.com/bethryansells

www.linkedin.com/pub/beth-ryan/2/918/a41/

PUNCHING DOUBT AND FEAR IN THE FACE

by Alan Young

My life was like a perfect Norman Rockwell painting. I was married, had three wonderful children, and was the associate pastor at my father's church. In January 2001, it all came to a screeching halt when my dad abruptly resigned during our board meeting.

I was shocked to say the least. I excused myself from the meeting to call my dear mother. "Mom," I said, "Did you know Dad was resigning from the church tonight?" She had no clue. I proceeded back to the meeting and tried to stop what was taking place. I knew something was not right, but he was determined. It was over; his 40 years of service to the Lord would conclude in three Sundays.

After that last week, I was in Temecula, CA at a skateboard park with my kids. I went out to the car to check my voice mail and saw my sister Joyce had left a message. With despair and urgency in her voice, she told me to, "Get up to Mom's right away!" I grabbed the kids, picked up my wife, and arrived at my mother's house about an hour and a half later. My sister was there with her kids and everyone was in tears, praying, and crying out to the Lord. My dad had left my dear mother a card saying he would do it all over again with her, that he loved her, but he was gone. Vanished. Disappeared.

After one week he returned. It was a family's worst nightmare. He told us that he had an affair with a lady from the church and she had conceived a child. Forty years of ministry and forty-four years of marriage were shattered. The church board asked me to pick up the torch and assume the role of senior pastor in place of my father, but I chose to flee from the situation. I wanted out. I ran from my calling.

So we left the ministry and moved back to North County, San Diego where I grew up. I had been in the ministry all of my adult life so I had to start at the bottom. I took sales jobs based on commission, selling credit card processing machines, timeshares, pre-need funerals, and RV's, so my income was very inconsistent. One of my managers at a time share resort told me I was too nice and honest to be a good salesman. We relied upon my wife's RN income.

We were doing just fine until the summer of 2003, when my wife ruptured three vertebrae catching a falling patient. Our income was immediately cut in half. Her injury resulted in a nine hour surgery three years later. Two weeks after the surgery she developed blood clots in her left leg and lungs which almost took her life. Life's struggles not only continued but began to mount. I reached out to ministers for their input and consolation, but alas, no help was found there. This led to further disillusionment and personal despair. One night I turned to the bottle for escape, which is totally out of character for me. Instead of escaping, I became consumed with anger and found myself shouting at God and ripping my Bible to shreds.

In reality, suicide was out of the question but not out of my thoughts. I vividly recall sitting alone in my living room, picturing ropes coming from the four corners of the walls and wrapping around my neck. I became jaded and developed a "woe is me" attitude. I said, "Lord I love You, but to hell with ministry. I will never preach again." This went on until the summer of 2006 when it was if the Lord hit me up side my head with a two-by-four. It wasn't an audible voice, it was that still small resounding voice of the Lord saying, "Alan, get over yourself and get back to what I have called you to do!" That day changed my life. I was back.

I truly thank God for the "desert times" because I am now 100% able to empathize with others. No matter what someone is going through, to be in a place where you cast no judgment, have only compassion and love, and listen with all ears is an incredible place to be. When the Lord restores, He restores big.

Because my father was in the ministry, visitors from all over the world would stay for weeks on end in our home. One man in particular, David Grant, had a profound impact on my life. He'd share his experiences working in India and talk about the mass amount of people living in utter poverty, people bound by the cast system with no way to escape, and the sex trafficking of women and children. I was moved to tears and knew as a young child that I would one day go to this great land. This was the beginning of my cause and purpose. You see, your cause will eventually consume you and when it does, you become like the sun, a blazing ball of energy that illuminates and brings life to a world of frozen hearts and suffering. My ambition in life was uprooted and replaced with a mission.

Matthew Barnett of the Los Angeles Dream Center is quoted as saying, "Mission is about the cause, and it doesn't take account of who gets the credit or fame. When you're invested in a mission, you submit to others, serve whenever possible, and stay engaged in the battle, no matter how difficult it becomes." I was motivated by ambition and walked away from my cause as a young man, then later in life, when the going got tough, I left the battle all together and looked for something easier to master, failing greatly and with dire consequences.

When I was 17, I lived on the North Shore of Oahu, surfing and living my dream, but I had fallen in a deep rut of substance abuse and was heading nowhere in a hurry. With the prompting of Tom Bauer of Surfing the Nations, I joined Youth With a Mission in Hawaii. within one year I was in India, and my life was transformed. I am now fully re-engaged in my cause and mission in life.

As the director of the Indian Sub-Continent for Agape International (www.Agape1040.com), I fly over 100,000 miles each year to Asia and across the US, encouraging, equipping, and ministering side by side with our Nepali Bhutanese pastors and leaders. We are establishing training centers via our Synergy School of Ministry, which is resulting in hundreds of new church plants in remote areas that have little to no witness of the Gospel. In the US, we help refugees adjust to their new life in their new country by setting up networks of support. Our ministry fights against human trafficking, systematically working to remove women and children from the horrors of sex slavery.

Having emerged out of personal pain and hardship, I thrive on giving back to others. Often, someone's cause is revealed at the lowest point of the valley, not the pinnacle of the mountain. I do this through speaking and personal blog at www.AlanYoung.org, which has a "punch doubt and fear in the face" attitude and initiates positive shifts which will bring change to your life.

Oh yeah, my mom and dad were remarried a few years later on the beach and are doing awesome!

ABOUT THE AUTHOR

Alan Young is a husband, father to three grown children, minister, and blogger. He's the Director of Agape International (Agape1040.com) for the Indian Sub-Continent and a sought after international speaker.

Alan is passionate about motivating others to fulfill their God given cause. His blogs offer words of encouragement and challenge others to dream often and dream big. AlanYoung.org is his personal blog with a "punch doubt and fear in the face" attitude that initiates positive shifts that will bring change into your life. Alan loves hanging out with family and friends, the outdoors, and surfing.

facebook.com/alan1040

twitter.com/_Alan_Young

www.linkedin.com/in/youngalan/

LEAVING AN IMPRINT

by Karli Grace

During junior college, I worked at a facility that provided developmentally disabled (DD) residential services for individuals who were labeled severe-profound, moderate, or educable. As a curious young employee, I once asked the resident psychologist, "Do you think that the severely, profoundly developmentally disabled have intelligence?"

He responded, "If they do, we don't know how to measure it yet."

I was certain these individuals had intelligence. I could sense and feel it. Still, there was no obvious way to get through to those who weren't able to walk, speak, or communicate in any way. Why did I feel that intelligence and potential existed, even though we couldn't tap it? I just had an inner knowing. Armed with that insight, I worked in that field for the next eleven years, developing techniques for reaching this population in meaningful ways.

For many years, the DD population existed in custodial care, warehoused and left to their own devices. You could find them wandering half naked in large open rooms, bodies and floors often covered in excrement. A significant shift led to the era of "tender loving care," and normalization and behavioral independent education programs began to emerge as I started my work in this field. It was great to be a part of this new era of treatment. Helping to successfully implement a Joint Commission on Accreditation of Hospitals process for a new facility was quite a feat. A behavioral approach with an interdisciplinary team of professionals was put in place, along with the problem-oriented record keeping system, policies, procedures, and support services. However, equally important for me was the small but monumental triumphs of residents under my aegis.

One man's situation always comes to mind. John was in his forties, ambulatory, non-verbal, and somewhat unsteady in his gait.

His main issue was that he didn't want to be touched or bothered in any way. During motor-music classes, I assisted John with the routine. He'd cross his arms and do his best to move away from me, twisting in one direction and then in another. I gently persisted that he move around the room, and I'd tap his tightly folded hands with the shakers. Tap, tap. Resist, resist.

The goal of the treatment was to improve gross motor skills through participation in the class. Two or three times a week we'd walk, run, step-up on a box and a balance beam, and work with shakers and rhythm. I say "we," but it was actually "me." I guided as I led the participants hand over hand through each step of each activity, one after the other, constantly saying the word representing the movement. This required constant positive reinforcement. "Good walking! Good stepping!" At times it was almost like whack-a-mole.

I'd finish a movement with one person and start the routine with the next. It took no time at all for each participant to stand up and move away from their seat. This left me to work with one person while re-seating those who popped up repeatedly.

"Good sitting!" It was strenuous, at best. Walk, walk. Run, run. Step, step. And so the class went. After six months of instructing this class, I had the surprise of my life. As I was walking with one participant, I turned around to see John step up to the balance beam and place his foot on it. He looked at me grinning ear to ear!

Wow! It took John six months to break down his barriers and independently respond to my consistent and steady expectation that he would complete my requests. I'm sure he was capable of completing all the routine tasks, but his fear prevented him from trusting me and himself. He no longer flinched when I used the shakers, but still remained somewhat resistant. John and I had established a relationship—a method of communicating that surpassed the imaginable. I was delighted at his breakthrough!

Unfortunately, I never had a chance to see if John made further progress. I left the facility shortly after his breakthrough, but to this day, I still marvel at the experience. I often wonder if he felt he lost a friend in me, or if he was even capable of noting my absence. Would John have been more responsive and productive if he'd had more than custodial care in his youth?

My approach included high expectations, believing that great progress was possible, and consistently working to promote the highest achievable outcome. I deeply believed in building on strengths and shifting weaknesses or minimizing their impact. As I think back to my question about intelligence, I now believe that I was able to tap into the very core of one's being: the intelligence, the life that I felt and that was the essence that I would call forth throughout my work. Although the DD population faced extreme mental, emotional, and often physical challenges, the behavioral treatment programs, combined with tender loving care, were able to bring about positive change for so many. These individuals were given a chance to maximize their potential.

This was the beginning of my over thirty year professional career, my insights into the potential of people, my belief in the impossible, and my passion to make life more personally rewarding for those with disabilities. Each subsequent career shift called upon what I'd learned and expanded my knowledge and experiential base. My mantra became, "How can I help a person or business entity know how much more potential exists?" If we are only using about ten per cent of our brain's capacity, then how much more are we capable of accomplishing? What gets in the way of those of us without the limitations of the developmentally disabled when we are so powerful?

Unfortunately, I dealt with middle school students who had been written off by many teachers. They were seen as the kids who were never going to make it. They set fires, bullied others, used drugs, or attempted suicide. Many were left to sit on the bench of life, never invited to join the team. They were made to feel that they were less than they really were.

Having dealt with all ages, life stages, and different populations, I have seen the adult version of the impact that erroneous childhood messages have left imprinted on the subconscious mind. People learn to shrink their value, diminish their self-confidence, live in fear, and hide their greatest dreams. In their own ways, they behave as John did in the motor- music class, resisting what life has to offer and afraid to trust anyone. They create and live in their own form of custodial care. Imprints can also be taken on after childhood. For example, we may develop a physical disability, chemical dependency, depression, suicidal or abusive behavior, or simply choose to become homeless during tough economic times. We take on and lock ourselves into silos of unworthiness, failure, or fear. We judge ourselves as not being good enough.

Life is ongoing change and we pass through many stages. Flow or resist. Choose to shift or be shifted. We spend so much time focusing from our negative imprints and what makes us different, when often, the worth, intrinsic value, and souls of people are what help us identify our power, potential, and what makes us all the same.

ABOUT THE AUTHOR

Karli Grace has dedicated her entire career to helping organizations and individuals harness their fundamental skill set to transcend the growth limitations we establish for ourselves. With a multi-disciplinary approach, Karli has developed practices and integrated systems that allow her clients to get to the center of their own personal "true north" and help them carve a plausible path to achievement. As both a strategist and a practical implementer, Karli has focused experience and sustainable case studies in the areas of human services; health/medicine; higher education; special education; ministry; publishing; retail; financial services; real estate; entrepreneurial ventures; and leisure, recreation, and therapeutic services.

To learn more about Karli, visit her website at:

karligrace.com

facebook.com/IamKarliGrace

twitter.com/IAmKarliGrace

www.linkedin.com/in/karligrace/

THE HEART OF A BLOGGER

Dan R. Morris

There wasn't much of a reason in the beginning. Doing what I do was a natural progression of my passion and what I'd spent years learning about in various jobs. I'm not sure how, but pretty much every job I'd ever had was better than the previous one. And nothing could be better than what I do now—it's the reason why I'm here.

In my previous life, I marketed an antioxidant nutritional supplement via TV and radio infomercials. My role included managing the content of the website. I used analytics, A/B tested pages, heat maps, surveys, and revenue to make decisions. I matched the message from the infomercial to the messaging on the web and most importantly, uncovered the commonalities between the longest subscribing customers in order to target more just like them. I also built small feeder websites which grabbed bits of niche search engine traffic and directed it to the product site, coordinating the messaging with the new audience and tracking the revenue. After the sale, I engaged in email marketing in order to determine how to build sales funnels to increase the stick rate, sell other products, and monetize referral networks.

It was glorious! Marketing, web, data, revenue… everything I loved all rolled into one, or so I thought.

One day I gave a speech on how to generate revenue online to a small group of bloggers. All the data-analyzing-gloriousness that had made me happy moments earlier fell flat. The audience's reaction to my speech was nothing less than life changing; for the first time, I realized that my "passion" was really about changing people's incomes and lives. While I loved figuring out how to sell more units, there was something about the gratitude and sincerity in the eyes of the people listening to my speech that just grabbed me. They weren't excited about selling more units; they were excited about changing their lives.

I believe that we build the prison in which we live. Our income level prevents us from reaching too deep, our ethics prevent us from straying too far, our fears prevent us from jumping too high, and our knowledge prevents us from risking too much. But for everyone who has expressed dismay about their situation, I remind you that there is freedom in this prison. You can find great happiness living inside these walls. You just have to realize that you've built the walls and you have the power to move them.

My speech forever altered the course of my life. Crunching numbers for a company would no longer provide me with joy and satisfaction. I now knew I had the ability to teach people how to move the walls of their prisons beyond the parameters of their dreams. And so my passion which provided yesterday's entertainment soon became the career that provided tomorrow's groceries for my family and for my clients.

I signed up for a blogging conference. If I was going to make this a career on my own I figured I'd better learn how to get the message out. I learned a lot about blogging, but the bulk of my time was spent with bloggers who were eager to learn a side of marketing that they hadn't previously thought much about. During the conference it became clear to me that my ability to expand and compliment their knowledge would change the way they "blogged" forever. It wasn't long before those bloggers were tweeting me their new Google rankings, traffic flow, and income levels. Again, they weren't excited about the numbers;

their enthusiasm stemmed from an understanding that their lives had changed for the better.

It's odd to think that my jobs at cemeteries, truck stops, restaurants, and baseball fields and my stints in real estate and the infomercial world would lead me to this. Somehow everything I'd done became the paradigm through which I could make bloggers shrewder and change lives.

Since the day I gave that speech, I have helped bloggers triple and quadruple their traffic, income, and love for their site. I've helped them publish books, negotiate TV deals, build their list with eBooks, sell their sites, and even build teams so they could just step away for a while. Some of my most important work has been teaching leverage. I show bloggers how to effectively harness the power of search engines so they don't have to be responsible for every visitor on their site. Leverage is teams, systems, procedures, and measurements—something business owners often learn too late.

Many bloggers also overlook the power of a housekeeper. When your two loves in life are family and work, having a few extra dollars to hire someone to manage the laundry and dishes can change relationships. While hiring a housekeeper doesn't necessarily mean you'll make more money, it does mean you can spend more time with the kids—something else I love helping bloggers accomplish.

What I love about the blogging community is that they don't need someone to do it for them; they just need to know how to do it correctly so they can be in charge of their success. Many have already built their teams and don't need to outsource to other firms. They just need the knowledge, the templates, and the methods of measuring success. An educated blogger is forever grateful. And, I might add, the most joyful self-starters to work with.

To reach bloggers, I travel the country speaking at blogging conferences, hold regional blogging workshops called "Blogging Concentrated" for advanced level marketers, and run a blogger education webinar series on Wednesday nights. I co-host an extremely active Facebook Group called FreeWeeklyMastermind, am the founder and author of CommonSenseRevenue.com, and write guest posts whenever I'm asked. I also offer one-on-one mastermind groups, consulting services, SEO, and even full-service marketing services.

If I see a concept or strategy that will make a blogger smarter, better, faster, and stronger, I endeavor to learn it or find someone who can teach it to my community. When one is smarter, we're all smarter. And while I work hard to help connect bloggers with brands, I've even had the opportunity to educate brands on working with bloggers. (Hey, that's just plain fun.)

I often hear people say that if you're doing what you love, you never have to work. I love the romanticized notion behind this idea, but the truth is, no matter how much you love what you do, there is always work to be done in your business. Being a successful entrepreneur isn't easy. It's easy to stay busy, but the hard part is being efficient enough to make an income and still have time to enjoy your family.

My name is Dan R. Morris. I make bloggers smarter so they can move their walls.

ABOUT THE AUTHOR

Dan R. Morris is the founder of <u>www. CommonSenseRevenue.com</u>, an enterprise dedicated to improving bloggers' revenue streams through their online efforts. Dan is an infomercial producer, niche website owner, product developer, author, and mastermind leader.

Dan takes his clients through a marketing discovery program that teaches them how to better optimize their video, images, audio, social media, and written online communication. The program also teaches bloggers how to effectively use and implement online tools such as analytics, annotations, testing, and sales funnels. Dan's goal is to help business owners become smarter, more efficient, and generate a sustainable income, and most importantly, spend more time with their families.

facebook.com/danrmorris
twitter.com/danrmorris
linkedin.com/in/danrmorris

CRACKPOT CREATIVITY

by Angela Wood

I t may sound strange, but my life and work is inspired by a pretty amazing parable penned by an anonymous writer. It goes a little something like this:

A water bearer had two large pots, one hung on each end of a pole, which he carried across his neck. One of the pots had a crack in it, but the other pot was perfect and always delivered a full portion of water. By the end of the long walk back to the house, the cracked pot arrived only half full. This occurred daily for two years, and the cracked pot grew increasingly ashamed of its imperfection. One day, the cracked pot lamented to the water bearer: "I am ashamed of myself and my inability to fulfill my role. This crack in my side causes water to leak all the way back to your house." The water bearer was filled with compassion and said, "My little friend, I have always known about your imperfection. I planted flower seeds on your side of the path. Every day while we walk back, you've watered them. You have brought beauty to the land."

I want to let you in on a little secret: My friends and family think I am a certified crackpot and for the most part I resemble that remark. In fact, that designation helps me justify my crazy compassion for the "least of these" and it also explains why I juggle my full-time responsibilities as a Web content manager and social media and marketing strategist for local companies, play league tennis, dance my heart out in my worship arts team, support domestic abuse survivors, and run my four kids from pillar to post without, I repeat...WITHOUT using performance enhancing drugs or consuming excessive amounts of Red Bull, Full Throttle, and Monster juice.

My sheer passion for life and all things cool and creative is the driving force that fuels my flame (okay, that sounds a little cheesy, but hopefully you get my drift). Perhaps it all started when my courageous mother enrolled me in every possible program that fostered creativity and critical thinking or when my grassroots politician father told me, "Make every occasion a great occasion for you know not when someone is taking your measure of faith to some higher place." Dad would be happy to know that ever since I graduated from Spelman in 1990 with an English degree, this California native has experienced some REALLY great occasions.

Topping the list are the years I taught English literature to snot-nosed middle and high school kids (no offense if one of those kids was yours). I relish the days I stood atop my desk a la Robin Williams in the movie, "Dead Poet's Society," and shouted at the top of my lungs the benefits of Shakespeare and the thrill of devouring great American classics. My students also had a chance to stand on their desks, shout, and learn without limits. I would love to think my passion for literature, film, Greek festivals, Harlem Renaissance parties, and disgust for grammatical formalities rubbed off on them. A few years ago, Redbook magazine said that I am a cross between Mary Poppins and a drill sergeant. I am pretty sure my students would agree.

After nine years bleeding composition papers, I made a tough decision: expand my horizons in order to utilize all my gifts and talents before becoming too old and too scared to try something new. God knows I didn't want to become one of those teachers who hates waking up in the morning and blames her discontent on the students or ruins their lives by forcing them to memorize useless facts and dumb them down with totally useless worksheets.

Like a crazy animal on steroids (and after enduring a short stint at Coke), I plunged head first into the dot.com world. What a ride! I witnessed some pretty amazing things and met a few of the most creative minds in the world—ideation experts, serial entrepreneurs, brand managers, research analysts, digital storytellers and more. I also saw a lot of money being poured down the drain on poorly planned and just plain stupid initiatives, but the lessons I learned were invaluable. I walked away from that experience, thinking, "Man, if I ever get a chance to run my own company, I'll jump at the chance."

A few years ago, something told me it was time to take the jump, forget the proverbial leap of faith. In order to fulfill my life's vision, I needed to take a quantum leap into the unknown. I needed to roll all my experiences together and use them to help others. I began by helping business owners manage their web copy, then with the advent of WordPress and other content management systems, I trained people how to build and maintain their own websites. It is so liberating to empower people to do for themselves what once took hours and hundreds of dollars to accomplish.

Then to my sheer delight, the social web emerged out of nowhere, and I began to become somewhat of a Web Hero, showing people how to connect with their customers, build better brands, and promote their business via Facebook, Twitter, YouTube, and LinkedIn. Everything began to move so quickly, and I was learning strategies that I could never glean from books. People began to ask me to speak about social media trends and viewed me as a valuable resource for all things Web 2.0.

As my client list expanded and the work in my Master's program became increasingly difficult, I discovered that I needed to rally the troops for help, and I had an epiphany: Why don't I train other "crack pots" like me to do what I do. There are so many people who would love to hire someone to set up their social media profiles, generate content for their blogs, live tweet for them at events, and create viral campaigns for them. Why don't I empower others by teaching them social media, content management, and online marketing skills so they can become successful marketing executives? Wouldn't it be a cool social experiment if my crackpot creativity rubbed off on digital natives and immigrants alike?

I decided to target cracked pots who fit into my "Four M's Model": retired or injured Military men and women eager to start their own businesses, Moms, Ministers, and Millennials—everyday heroes who are not afraid to roll up their sleeves and work hard, individuals who are innovative and want to revolutionize the world one idea at a time, and young outcasts who have gotten in trouble or been rejected by society, but who are not afraid to turn it around and use disruptive thinking to create a little wonder on the web. These are the people who I run to when clients need someone to update their websites, set up e-tail stores, conduct WordPress training sessions, create social media campaigns, live tweet at events, create Facebook campaigns, write blog posts, guest vlog, or develop super fantastic t-shirts that engage and delight. These folks are my "Digital Go-to Group." They help me answer the question I am asked over and over again: How can I use social media to make money on the web? They are my crackpots who cause flowers to bloom everywhere they go and love them.

ABOUT THE AUTHOR

Angela Wood is an ideation specialist, social media trainer, and Web Hero with an incredible ability to conceptualize and turn thoughts into action. As the owner of Wonderfish Creative Solutions, a brand consultancy specializing in helping small to mid-size businesses develop strong brands that resonate with their target audiences, Angela is committed to putting "joy and wonder back in business."

Her passion for technology and people perfectly positions her to help companies that want to attract fans who enthusiastically support and brag about their brands. The California-native and relocated southern belle is recognized as an innovative thought leader experienced in the coordination of multiple media projects, online community development, social networking, and corporate imaging.

Check them out at www.wonderfishworldwide.com, and join the cracked pot revolution.

www.facebook.com/angela.wood.7334

www.twitter.com/gowonderfish

HOW TO WRITE A BOOK WITH VIRTUALLY NO EXPERIENCE

by Marijo Tinlin

W hen I was young I wrote fictional stories about living in Colorado, a far away, mystical place to a girl from Kansas City. After I moved to Denver years later, I located those stories and every single one of them was about Colorado. How ironic that my life-long dream of writing a book would materialize in the very place I wrote about as a girl.

While I did major in journalism at the University of Kansas, after graduation I went into the business side of publishing—circulation. For years, I managed circulation for magazines and then moved into database sales. That's about as far away from writing as you can get while still working in publishing!

I traveled, made a lot of money, and sold names and addresses to businesses so they in turn could sell those people more stuff. After a series of life-altering events, God used His divine intervention and brought me back to what I had always wanted to do—write a book. But how? After years of not writing a word beyond a business email, how could I write a book?

It was just about this time that I finally discovered Twitter and started building my first website, Teaching Your Toddler (www. teachingyourtoddler.com). I bought all the books I could find on websites and social media to educate myself with the ins and outs. That's when I discovered that Joel Comm literally lived right down the road from me. The guru of Twitter and AdSense lived just 40 miles away.

When he Tweeted that he needed some editorial help for his website, Family First (www.familyfirst.com), one of the oldest family-oriented websites on the Internet which has a great deal of "cred" among the millions upon millions of bloggers, I jumped at the chance to finally write. I was a work-at-home mom with five kids and I needed something for myself. I'm a mom who loves to write—a family site was a perfect fit. I tweeted Joel and mailed him my resume. We met and I served as his editor-in-chief for several years.

As editor, I had the opportunity to interview amazing people including experts, celebrities, and authors. It was such a blast! I had always thought it would be fun and interesting to interview different types of people, but I never knew how to go about it. Now I had a venue.

One summer, I interviewed actress Janine Turner about her foundation, Constituting America (www.constitutingamerica.org). The sole mission of CA is to educate Americans, especially kids, about our Constitution and what it means. My angle was to talk to Janine about how she instilled patriotism in her teenage daughter Juliette. As I was conducting the interview, the thought occurred to me that there must be more stories about how parents and organizations are instilling patriotism in our children. They don't learn much about it in school. Heck, some schools don't even say the Pledge of Allegiance anymore. Why not try to write a book about how great our country is and the importance of instilling patriotism in our children?

The question was how. Which brings me back to Joel Comm. He was the one and only best-selling author I knew at the time. He had to know more about book publishing than I did, so I pitched him my idea of compiling a book of interviews with famous Americans who take pride in our country and how they instilled patriotism in their own kids. Apparently, he thought it was a good idea because the next message I got was from David Hancock, CEO and Founder of Morgan James Publishing, the publisher of this book. David asked me to write a brief summary of my concept so he could take it to the board for a final decision. They said yes to my proposal and I was off and running.

The first thing I had to do was find people to talk to me. I had a publisher, which was good, because although authors usually write their books before a publisher says yes to publishing or publish the book themselves, in this case I needed to prove to my famous interviewees that I was legitimate as I was not an established author.

I started networking like crazy! I compiled a huge list of everyone I could think of who might be patriotic and started working it. I started asking the "connectors," those who seem to know everyone or at least someone who knows someone, if they could arrange a meeting. Through one of my contacts and a series of her friends, I got my first "yes" from Rachel Campos-Duffy, one of the first reality TV stars, occasional co-host of "The View," and wife to Congressman Sean Duffy of Wisconsin. I was elated!

I back-tracked through the interviews I had conducted for Family First to determine if there was a proud American who would be willing to contribute and found Debbie Lee. She's the founder of America's Mighty Warriors and a Gold Star Mom. Debbie raised the ultimate patriot, Marc Allan Lee, the first SEAL killed in Iraq. She said yes. Phew! As with everyone I spoke to, I asked her if there was anyone else she knew who would be willing to speak with me. The long and the short of it is, Debbie led me to Erick Erickson, editor of RedState, who was kind enough to put me in touch with Ed Meeses's office. Ed Meese served as Attorney General under Ronald Reagan and with Erick's permission to use his name, I got the interview, which is definitely one of the highlights of my life, by the way.

I Tweeted Tea Party speaker and radio host Kevin Jackson about my book and got a call from his assistant minutes later. He in turn connected me with Reverend Steven Craft, a former prison minister who had overcome drug addiction and other challenges to graduate from Harvard and become a great public speaker. From an off-handed comment made during an interview with Renaissance man Seth Swirsky about his latest album, I realized how much he loves our country and he became a part of the book. And so on.

I received a lot of "no's" but many of those rejections turned into great connections. I was connected to Ginni Thomas, wife of Supreme Court Justice Clarence Thomas, who did not interview but taught me about "blurbs." She blurbed my book and appears on the back cover. I spoke to the public relations representatives for Bill O'Reilly, Senator Fred Thompson, and Congressman Paul Ryan, although they didn't contribute. I even found Sarah Palin's publicist, who was supportive, but in the middle of writing her own book and couldn't contribute. When I was tracking down Sean Hannity, I got the name of one of the producers of "Fox & Friends" and eventually scored an interview on the show after the book was published. Again, another highlight of my life. Although many great Americans said no, at least I got connected to them.

So, my writing career began in a circuitous way, but it did begin a journey that continues today, full of great friends, amazing connections, and wonderful stories to tell.

ABOUT THE AUTHOR

Marijo Tinlin is a wife, mother, author, missionary, business expert, and entrepreneur. She is the author of, *How to Raise An American Patriot, Making it Okay for Our Kids to Be Proud to Be American*, which includes 13 interviews with patriotic Americans. She also blogs for several outlets and is the co-founder of Personal

Protection Plans (www.personalprotectionplans.org), a site that teaches people what to do during critical events in their homes or businesses.

www.facebook.com/raisinganamericanpatriot

twitter.com/mnewtontinlin

www.linkedin.com/in/marijotinlin/

THE "DUCT TAPE" METHOD
by Antoine McCoy

P eople often ask me how a city boy from Bronx, New York who graduated from an Ivy-League school ends up teaching struggling students in public school. That probing question always fascinates me because the simple answer is…why not?

Here's why I teach:

Mr. McCoy,

Thanks for being such an awesome teacher. You teach things to me in a way I could understand. And that means so much to me. :) I've never been this good in math and for once I'm proud of myself.

Thanks. It sucks I won't be able to see you next year. One because I passed this class and two because I'm moving, but I won't forget you.

This was a note one of my high school students recently slipped incognito on my desk after the bell rang. I quickly read it, ran to the door, and yelled for the student to come back so I could talk to her.

"Thanks so much for the note," I exclaimed. "That really means a lot to me, as your teacher and case manager. So, you're moving?" She

126

proceeded to tell me that she may be moving out of the state with her mom and siblings and how she was excited, yet sad at the same time. She told me how she was nervous to take Algebra I next year as she had never been good at math. I reassured her that she was ready and a star student in my class. I explained to her that her lack of self-confidence would be the only barrier to her success in math, not her lack of ability.

I told her she was one of my favorite students because she had a caring heart and other students were drawn to her. I told her that she was a leader and that I was proud of her for expressing herself through her dyed hair, lip piercings, and quirky hats she wore to class. I asked her what she wanted to do with her life and what she was good at. With a huge smile and wide-eyed she answered, "I love to write stuff like poetry and short stories, and I might want to do hair and nails and things like that."

"You mean, Cosmetology?"

"Yeah, what you said," she responded with a laugh.

"You know, you can be a writer and take your poetry and short stories and have them published in a book? And you can do hair and nails to support yourself while you pursue your writing career."

"Reeeeaaaally?" she said.

"Yes, reeeaaally. Start small and build from there. Write your poems in a notebook and think about starting your own blog." She hung on every word I spoke like she had just entered Narnia or Wonderland. It was like a whole new world of possibilities had opened up to her. I informed her that I was also a writer and was in the process of writing a book for parents and teachers which would provide advice and tips for how to motivate their kids to realize their potential and help them become more involved in their lives.

"Oh, that's really good, Mr. McCoy. That's really cool."

I also told her that I had a blog under my name, AntoineMcCoy. com, that started out as a site to help other teachers, but now supports and helps both parents and teachers motivate, inspire, and encourage the next generation to fulfill their dreams.

"Hey, I have to let you go to your next class, but do you have a notebook to jot down your ideas when you get a spark of genius?" I asked.

"No."

I handed her a red spiral notebook then went into my file cabinet and took out my yellow spiral notebook. "This is where I put all my ideas and the steps I need to take to make them happen. Now this is your very own book to capture your thoughts, feelings, and ideas. Guard it with your life," I said with a serious, but joking smile. "I want you to know that I'm proud of you and wherever you might end up, don't stop fighting for your dreams, OK? You may get a lot of resistance while pursuing them, but guess what—that comes with the territory.

Every great person who has made an impact on the world faced resistance. Some people didn't like what they said or what they did, but guess what—that's OK. You don't have to please everyone and those who like what you have to offer will follow you."

Parents often ask me, "How do I motivate my child to do anything and care about their future." In other words, how can they get their disengaged child to become more engaged. When I hold conferences with parents, I offer them advice and practical tips on ways to get their child or teen motivated and more involved in school, family life, and their community. I tell them that motivating and engaging kids is all about building relationships and connecting. One of the best ways to do this is to actively listen to them.

I call this active listening strategy the "duct tape" method. I find that when kids tell us what motivates, frustrates, and encourages them, adults often judge and dismiss what they are saying. This breaks the connection between the adult and child, often making the child more distant and disengaged. So, here's a simple way to employ the "duct tape" method and get some immediate results. First, ask your kid a question. One simple, yet powerful question to ask is, "How can I be a better parent to you?" Next, imagine yourself taking a thick, long strip of duct tape and applying it to your mouth so that you are unable to speak. Then, really LISTEN to what your child is saying without any judgment, whether right or wrong in assessing your parenting skills.

Try to hone in on your child's perceptions of you as a parent; if the way your child sees you is the very opposite of how you want to be seen, be intentional about changing a few things. Their perception, whether right or wrong, is their reality. They will be motivated to connect with you based upon that reality.

For some, the hardest part is not saying anything or thinking of a justification for your actions while your child is speaking. Therefore, physically applying a piece of duct tape may be necessary. If you choose to go this route, both you and your child will get a laugh and turn a potential uncomfortable moment together into one that is light-hearted and playful. Try it for yourself.

I love teaching, motivating, and inspiring kids to live passionate lives and realize their God-given potential. I also get a thrill from equipping parents and teachers to do the same through my products and services (books, workshops, speaking engagements, and coaching).

ABOUT THE AUTHOR

Antoine McCoy is a teacher, writer, speaker, and educational entrepreneur. He is an expert at motivating and inspiring kids to discover their passions and maximize their God-given potential. As a Nationally Board Certified K-12 teacher, he works with students who have learning, behavioral, emotional, and social difficulties in and outside of the classroom. Antoine is passionate about equipping and supporting parents, teachers, community leaders, volunteers, and others who work with children with the tools and resources they need to help the next generation succeed. You can learn more about Antoine and his products and services at antoinemccoy.com.

www.facebook.com/AntoineMccoyOnline
twitter.com/antoinemccoy
www.linkedin.com/in/antoinemccoy

IT'S NOT HOW MUCH YOU KNOW, IT'S HOW MUCH YOU CARE

by Brad Dixon

had what some would say was a "charmed childhood." My parents were not extremely wealthy but we certainly had enough. I remember growing up in that small Iowa town during the summer, mowing lawns and going to the monthly ice cream social where the old guys played music in the gazebo, the sky was full of fireflies, and everyone shared their latest homemade ice cream creation. I remember those days like yesterday; it seemed like summer went on forever, fall turned the trees into a kaleidoscope of color, followed by fluffy white snowdrifts waiting for the beautiful flowers of spring to appear and start the whole process over again. I had a wonderful home and a wonderful family. B as so many know, kids can be rough.

Because we lived comfortably, I was seen as the little rich kid. I had no friends and I actually would be sick every morning at the thought of facing school every day. This had a lasting effect on my self-worth. I started my own company at the age of eight. My parents drove me sixty miles into the big city every fall so I could buy my sample products. I would get a business loan from my father and pay him back out of my profits. I had a big ugly green suitcase in which I packed all my samples. I lugged that heavy suitcase all over town, going door-to-door selling my wares. "Would you like to buy my Christmas gifts, Christmas cards, and Christmas wrapping"?

Between mowing lawns and my Christmas card business, in two years I had saved up enough money to buy a big three wheel ATV. I was the envy of all the kids and suddenly had a few more friends. It was this early entrepreneurship that really captivated me and structured the remainder of my life. I studied ministry, but that didn't really work out, and I carried a self-imposed guilt of failure with me for a long time.

This mindset controlled my life for almost twenty-five years. My negativity and guilt was further amplified by a failed marriage and eventual divorce. The mind is the most powerful tool we possess. It must be protected, preserved, and nourished with positive thoughts 24/7. It took me a long time to realize that focus is everything. If you focus on the positive, it will come; if you focus on the negative, that too will come.

I began my Internet marketing business back in 1998, the early days of online entrepreneurship. We developed a membership site, which offered hundreds of products and did very well. From 2002–2003 we got hacked four times by Chinese and Russian web attacks. It was very costly; I lost most of my members and my confidence. I threw in the towel. These were dark days for me. I went from one sales job to another, from customer service to restaurant management.

Then my life began to take a turn. I joined a men's accountability group which focused on taking responsibility and finding our passions. I had heard of the concept of accountability but had never experienced anything like this. I cannot even begin to express the importance of an accountability group. I realized I had two passions: running my own business and working with children. I had always been involved with the youth activities at my church, teaching children object lessons and storytelling. Thus my career as a teacher began. I substitute taught for two years while completing my teaching certification. It was an incredible amount of work but very rewarding. After teaching for only two years, I once again found myself without a job due to state funding issues.

I was in the process of becoming a different person, or perhaps returning to the person I started out as. Through the eyes of my accountability group, I began to understand how to live out your passions. During this time, I had been watching and learning as the Internet evolved. When I thought the moment was right, I began another online business—new and improved. I quickly grew my customer base, which brought with it its own set of headaches. I now had a family to support and my passion became earning a living for our survival. I was so overwhelmed with creating the next great product and maintaining a steady flow of cash that my customer service was shoddy at best. The stress of providing for a family was my focus, but stress can never be your focus if you intend to be successful. I had burned bridges with existing customers through my poor service. It was not intentional, but life happens and instead of reaching out for help, I buried my head in the sand and ignored things. As you can imagine, the very thing I was focused on, money, eluded me.

Through the various groups I was involved with, I discovered that there were many other people who were trying to figure out how to survive just like I was. I began to literally reinvent myself. I realized my real passion was helping others. Zig Ziglar said, "If you help enough other people get what they want, you will always get what you want." I grew up listening to guys like Zig Ziglar, Tony Robbins, Anthony Hopkins, and John Maxwell, so I knew the right things to do, but life got in the way.

It was difficult at first, helping others without expecting anything in return. How would I pay the bills; what will happen next. I began to retrain my brain to my old ways of thinking: giving without expecting anything in return, providing the fastest and best service possible, and doing what was right because it was right. That became my focus: helping others find their passion and showing them how to become successful doing what they love.

I am now 50, half a century old. That sounds really ancient when you say it that way. I have wasted so much of my life focusing on the negative. It would be easy to dwell on it and most people do. No matter what your religious affiliation, I believe these two statements from the Bible are universal truths: "As a man thinks in his heart, so is he," and, "The power of life and death is in the tongue." I am a prime example of the consequences of a negative mindset.

The genius next door, it is not about your IQ. It is about living a life of focus and passion. Those around you can be your biggest downfall. They mean well but they're scared, trying to survive, living life without passion. Choose your friends wisely, get an accountability group and live a life of passion, helping others and making a difference. It took me a long time to come back to what I knew as a young entrepreneur.. What is your genius? What is your passion? What will you do with it?

ABOUT THE AUTHOR

Online Reputation Management & Marketing Specialist, Business Growth Strategist, Author and Professional Speaker, **Brad Dixon** has spent the better part of forty years in the art of selling and customer service. He began his first successful company at the age of eight and has created several companies as well as worked for a number of major Fortune 100 companies. He is a former teacher, online entrepreneur, and author of the book, Giving Away the Farm to Pay off the Mansion.

He built a number of successful businesses by focusing on the needs of others and helping them achieve their goals. He currently serves as President of a multinational company now serving over 800 clients in thirty countries. The motto of his life and company have been "Carbon Copy Success". He studies what is successful and patterns his business after it.

To learn more about Brad, visit <u>BradDixonOnline.com</u>.
www.facebook.com/braddixononline
twitter.com/ccstudionews
www.linkedin.com/pub/brad-dixon/38/593/a47

LEADING WITH ACCEPTANCE

by Nancy Rose

As a child, I felt misunderstood and unaccepted for who I was—a strong, feisty girl with intense feelings and tenacious persistence. Out of five children, I was regarded as the "difficult" one. Although I never doubted that my mother loved me, she didn't seem to like me very much, and this wounded me deeply. Each day, I tried anew to get on her good side, but our explosive clashes left her exhausted and desperate, wondering out loud, "Why can't you just be like the others?"

This question filled me with shame. I couldn't change who I was, so I tried to stifle the characteristics and tendencies that got me into trouble. I hated being cast as the squeaky wheel, the needy one, the greedy one, so I did my best to keep my feelings to myself and just go with the flow. My only saving grace was my intelligence. My family also considered me as "the smart one," which made me feel valued. I channeled all of my drive and intensity into academics and lived in a "trance of accomplishment" until my mid-twenties. One day I realized I'd become a tax attorney and CPA so my mom would like me—an excruciating but liberating realization. I could finally stop chasing after my mom's approval and start healing myself and hopefully, our relationship.

135

A deeper awakening came six years later when my first child, Jordan, was born. From day one, he was intense, tenacious, and passionate. Despite the depth of my love for him, I noticed how often I wished he was different. It dawned on me that a generation earlier, this is how my mother felt about me and I was instantly filled with a new-found compassion for her and what I put her through. At the same moment, I knew that I had to do everything in my power to make sure I didn't cause my son the kind of pain I had endured. I vowed to find a way to understand and accept Jordan for who he was and never make him feel ashamed of being himself.

It took many years of trial and error and an in-depth study and understanding of acceptance, but I knew I was on to something. I was able to heal my relationship with my mother and raise my two sons to be exactly who they are. Together, my sons, my mother, and I ended a toxic legacy that threatened our well-being and that of future generations. I learned to lead with acceptance, and as I shared my philosophy and techniques with family and friends, their feedback confirmed that I had something powerful to offer struggling families.

Maya Angelou once said, "As soon as healing takes place, go out and heal somebody else." Heeding these words of wisdom, I began my journey with a commitment to help others lead with acceptance.

In modern-day parenting, lack of acceptance is the elephant in the room. Amidst the avalanche of parenting advice and techniques available, the overall message advocates compliance. But children misbehave for a reason, and if they don't feel understood and accepted, no technique or chart is going to solve the problem. It's like putting a Band-Aid on an open wound: it's not effective.

Children have a fundamental need to be seen and accepted for who they are. Yet somewhere along the line we've lost sight of this basic human need in our parenting techniques. Kids grow up afraid to be themselves because they are under the impression that they need to be a certain way to be loved. Compliant kids go along with the program, traveling the path to "success" as defined by their parents. What about the defiant ones? They're criticized for things they can't change and start to repress their feelings, which makes them angry and they either rebel or swallow their anger and suffer.

Our culture certainly plays a part in this tragedy. We live in a competitive and uncertain world where parents understandably encourage their children to become successful, albeit sometimes putting undue pressure and expectations on them. When this happens, our efforts to support our children are misguided. We push them to excel in as many areas as possible and demonstrate excellence across the board so they can get into the best schools and gain advantages. The irony is that in an attempt to ensure our children's success, we frequently ignore the one thing that will practically guarantee their lifelong well-being: acceptance of who they are at their core.

When acceptance is the focal point of parenting, families are able to build a warm, solid, connected, and lasting foundation for a relationship of mutual respect. Feeling appreciated and understood for who we are puts us on the path to authentic success because we are comfortable in our own skin, aware of both our gifts and challenges, and confident to share our unique talents with the world. Sadly, the opposite is also true: feeling as if no one understands us for who we are affects us at the deepest level and leaves us wounded. We tuck away parts of who we are to avoid rejection and seek approval wherever we can find it.

So why aren't we, as parents, as a society, making acceptance a parenting priority? Perhaps it's because acceptance is a difficult concept to define. Most parents would agree that we should accept our children for who they are, but in the day-to-day trenches of parenting, what does this mean? I decided to write a book based on my own experiences called, *Raise the Child You've Got—Not the One You Want*, in order to help parents understand what they must accept and what they can change. By following a new model of parenting called "Leading with Acceptance," parents can avoid lifelong battles, raise happy and thriving children, and gain peace of mind. "Leading with Acceptance" offers parents, for the first time, the resources they need to understand and accept who their child truly is.

"Leading with Acceptance" means accepting your children's "CoreSelf," which is the starting point of building a loving, respectful connection. This foundation will set the stage for you to become a leader who teaches values, morals, and standards of right and wrong, which will guide your children's behavior and help them become successful using the gifts they were given.

The CoreSelf is made up of nine innate temperament traits that remain stable over a lifetime:

1. Activity,
2. Adaptability,
3. Distractibility,
4. Ease with the unfamiliar,
5. Intensity,
6. Optimism,
7. Persistence,
8. Regularity, and
9. Sensory reactivity.

With this foundation of acceptance, you are in a position to genuinely influence your child as he or she matures, rather than holding a position of power that is unsustainable and breeds resentment and alienation.

ABOUT THE AUTHOR

Nancy Rose is an author, speaker, and parenting coach from Napa, California. As a self-proclaimed "Acceptance Advocate," the former tax attorney and CPA speaks to groups of parents, educators, and change-makers, raising awareness of the importance of accepting children for who they are, not who parents want them to be. Her book, *Raise the*

Child You've Got—Not the One You Want, teaches parents how to lead with acceptance in order to stop battling, start connecting with their children, and enjoy parenting peace of mind. To learn more about Nancy's method, visit her website, www.nancyjrose.com.

facebook.com/pages/Raise-the-Child-Youve-Got-Not-the-One-You-Want-by-Nancy-Rose/149300688539666

twitter.com/NancyRoseTweets

www.linkedin.com/in/rosenancy/

THE INVESTING CODE
by Brian Ochsner

I t's not easy to find a safe place to invest your money AND get a decent rate of return. You probably remember the good old days of the late nineties stock market boom in which almost any stock with tech, telecom, or Dot.com in its name was a golden ticket for investors.

Maybe it was in the mid-2000's when real estate values went up by 10-20% a year and you could easily refinance your house, get a mortgage, and extract tens of thousands of dollars out at a time (and because it was borrowed money, it was tax-free!). Those were the days. But the stock market has crashed twice in the past thirteen years, and sometimes when people are "once bitten, twice shy," they are hesitant to get back in the market. If you fit this description, I don't blame you a bit. I've done a little short-term trading in the stock market, and frankly, I'm not a great stock trader. I've been much better at predicting longer-term trends in the past ten years.

Back in 2003, I noticed that our Federal Reserve and government were borrowing, printing, and spending money just like governments have done in centuries past, and so I became very bullish on gold and silver. In hindsight it was a good call, as both markets have tripled since then. In 2004, I wrote a guest commentary on PrudentBear.com, explaining that the residential real estate boom didn't have the solid fundamentals to support it and this bull market would eventually end. Americans' incomes weren't going up at the same rate as home values, and the low interest rates and super-easy credit wouldn't last forever. In 2007, the sub-prime mortgage showed signs of weakness, and that was the beginning of the end of the real estate boom. In January 2008, I thought bad times were ahead for quasi-government entities Fannie Mae and Freddie Mac. They were a primary reason for the real estate boom, as they bought mortgages from Wells Fargo, Washington Mutual, and other lenders then bundled them into mortgage-backed securities and sold them to hedge funds, institutional investors, and even foreign governments such as China and Russia.

Why was I bearish (negative) on Fannie and Freddie? I went to Yahoo Finance to look at both companies' financial statements, but the statements for the last three quarters were missing! If they weren't quasi-government entities, there's no way they would have gotten away with this without the stock price plunging, and/or corporate executives paying fines or doing jail time. How did I plan to profit on Fannie and Freddie's missing financial statements? I bought put options with a February and April expiration. When you buy a put, you're betting that the company's stock price will go down and the value of the put will go up. Unfortunately, Fannie and Freddie's stock price didn't go down far enough (and fast enough) to make money, and both options expired worthless. Several months later, my prediction was proven correct. On September 9, 2008, both Fannie Mae and Freddie Mac were placed into government receivership and taken over by the federal government.

I'm not telling you these stories to brag or pat myself on the back but as proof that I know what I'm talking about when it comes to finance and investing. I also graduated with Bachelors' Degrees in accounting and agribusiness from Kansas State University, passed the CPA Exam on my third attempt, and worked as an accountant and financial analyst for over seven years.

Even though I have what seems like a great financial background, it wasn't very helpful when learning how to become a successful investor. On a cold, snowy February night in 2000, I went to a Barnes & Noble and came across a prominently displayed book with a purple cover: *Rich Dad, Poor Dad,* by Robert Kiyosaki. I devoured the book from cover to cover in two days, and it started my quest to discover how people become great investors. I call myself a "recovering financial junkie," because I spent so much time and effort learning about almost every kind of investment under the sun, more than any normal human being should. I took courses on stock trading and residential real estate, studied economic trends and history, and learned the difference between Keynesian and Austrian economics (don't worry, you don't have to know that). I've also traded stocks and options occasionally since 2001. Through this self-education, I've realized that growing (and protecting) your wealth isn't quite as easy as "buy low and sell high." You also have to know when to buy and sell—it doesn't have to be timed perfectly—even experienced investors find it almost impossible to buy at the lowest point and/or sell at the highest.

Investing isn't as easy as your stockbroker or financial planner tells you it is. You've probably heard this phrase (or some variation of it) from a financial salesperson explaining her investment philosophy: "Spread out your money into a well-diversified portfolio of stocks, bonds, and mutual funds over the long-term and you'll be fine." Unfortunately, that's been the worst investment advice possible since 2000. You probably discovered that this investment advice was nothing more than a feel-good sales pitch that was in your adviser's best financial interest—not yours. Financial planners and stockbrokers are very good salespeople but extremely bad investors.

Every investment is affected by different factors, or dimensions, that you need to be aware of before you decide to put your hard-earned money into it. You probably want me to give you the "easy button" for investing, or something like, "Three easy steps to investing for retirement." Believe me, if I had those kind of magical powers, I'd gladly grant that wish. You'd be rich and happy, and I'd be a very, very wealthy man. Unfortunately, there's no easy button or easy road to investment riches.

Here's what you need to know about investment markets for the foreseeable future: There is no such thing as a safe, secure place or "risk-free way" to invest your money. That includes keeping cash in the bank or under the mattress. Whether it's stocks, bonds, rental real estate, commodities such as gold and silver, or day-trading in FOREX and other online markets (and even keeping cash in your pocket), every investment has a degree of risk and potential downside. There's also a degree of manipulation in every market; unfortunately, there's no such thing as a "free" market anymore.

If you would've talked to me about "manipulated markets" in years past, I would have brushed it off as "conspiracy theory" talk and lumped you in with the crazy folks who wear tinfoil hats and talk about black helicopters. After plenty of due diligence and research, I came to the undeniable conclusion that wealthy investors and big financial institutions (and yes, even governments) have a hand in guiding American and world financial markets. If you don't believe me, read Matt Taibbi's recent articles in *Rolling Stone* about the rigging of the LIBOR and crude oil markets. On April 25,2013, the headline read: "Everything Is Rigged: The Biggest Price-Fixing Scandal Ever."

So how do you invest in a world where markets are rigged and financial salespeople aren't any help? I offer people a free report titled "How to Protect and Grow Your Wealth Without a Stock Broker or Financial Planner.", which you can find at www.TheInvestingCode. com. While brokers and planners may hate me for writing this report, I think it's time you discovered what factors can affect your investments and how you can become a better-informed and wealthier investor.

ABOUT THE AUTHOR

Brian Ochsner is a former accountant and current financial blogger, economic analyst and direct-response copywriter. Through over 12 years of research and study of economic trends, financial cycles and history, he's discovered a framework that non-financial people can use to make better investment decisions.

With this information, Brian called the bull market in gold and silver in 2003… forecast the residential real estate bust three years ahead of time in 2004… and saw the downturn of Freddie Mac and Fannie Mae in early 2008. One of his life goals is to increase financial and economic literacy in North America and around the world.

He lives in the Denver-metropolitan area and enjoys golf, poker and the Colorado outdoors in his spare time. You can read his financial blog at PrudentOx.Blogspot.com, and his website at www.TheInvestingCode.com.

www.linkedin.com/in/brianochsner

KOOL-AID LABELS
AND CANDY

by Mary Hladio

I come from a family of entrepreneurs. My mom was a social worker who started her own agency. Her side of the family was extremely innovative about their circumstances—whatever they may be. Their motto was, "I know what I want, and I'm going to go after it myself!" It was inevitable that this entrepreneurial spirit would have an effect on me.

My mom loves to tell the story about how when I was little, I would hold "garage sales" in my room. I would go through my things, decide what I didn't need, put my desk at my door, and sell things to my little brothers. And they would buy them!

Another story that my mom likes to tell is about how I saved up Kool-Aid labels to fund a lemonade stand. When I was a kid, Kool-Aid ran a promotion in which they would send you a lemonade stand in return for 100 labels. I was so obsessed with getting that stand that I collected labels not only from our house, but from my grandma, our neighbors, and my mom's nonprofit firm.

When I finally got my stand, I sold lemonade, iced tea, and cherry Kool-Aid. Eventually I expanded into the popsicle business by freezing drinks in little Dixie cups. It wasn't long before I was coming up with ways to create an enterprise. I would go to the store with my mom and ask her if she would buy penny candy so that I could resell it. The candy racket taught me one of my first lessons in basic economics. If I bought candy for a penny and resold it for two pennies, what was the incentive for kids to pay double the price when they could just go to the store and get it for cost? Location! I became the neighborhood store—kids didn't have to go down to the corner because I was right there hocking my wares from a more convenient location next door.

For a couple of summers on the weekends I'd set up my little stand, and that's when my mom taught me my next lesson. She said, "You're taking all of the profits, but you haven't paid any of your expenses yet." I asked her what she meant, and she said, "I purchased the Kool-Aid, so you owe me money for it, and whatever you have left over is your profits. You can't take all of the revenues." I was so bummed when she told me that! I remember thinking that she was cheating because she was going to buy the Kool-Aid anyway. I thought I was just using the resources that were at my disposal.

My entrepreneurial fixation continued to grow as I got older. When I was in my early teens, I wasn't allowed to go to the local dances so I decided I would hold a dance. I found a community center, conducted a cost-price analysis, and hired a DJ (who was my cousin). I made flyers, charged five bucks at the door, and sold soda and chips inside. My mom even wanted to get in on it. She decided she was going to set up a stand selling hotdogs. I didn't like this idea because it felt like she was invading my territory! I remember having the same discussion that she had with me about the Kool-Aid. I told her that she owed me a finder's fee for booth rental. And she did! She gave me ten bucks.

My family did this kind of stuff all the time. We had these ideas that would start out small but always turned into something bigger.

The next thing you know, you'd be in a costume doing a tap dance trying to sell something.

When I graduated from college, I eventually landed a job at an accounting firm. One of the partners asked me if I was interested in computers. PCs were just starting to show up on people's desks—those big honkin' 286's and 386's. I downloaded some material and learned how to conduct IT audits. My first one was pretty successful, and the partner convinced me that I should start my own small firm. My first "real" business was called Global Systems Solutions. My brother had just graduated and he became one of my first employees. We set up the computers and servers in mom and pop shops.

We got a license from Unisys to sell servers, and I did that for about eighteen months. But the problem was, I wasn't really ready to own my own company. Today when I evaluate companies I work with, I always ask them about their organizational structure, mission, and vision. Some of that stems from my own trials with my first company; I didn't have those basic building blocks in place yet.

I learned a few other lessons that helped me understand company owners today. When my brother came on board, I remember getting into an argument with him about roles and responsibilities. He wasn't happy because I wasn't introducing him with a certain title. But my feeling was, "It's my company! My name is on the certificate, it's my castle, or rather, my loan. And while your opinion matters, it doesn't matter here!"

I work with owners now who feel like it's their company, their baby. If someone tells them what or how to do something, they don't like it. That's why I decided to work with mid-sized companies. When I'm sitting in the conference room listening to their stories, it doesn't matter what industry they're from, I understand them. I've been dealing with family-run companies my entire life, including those within my own family!

There are many resources, such as business coaches, courses, and networking groups, for small companies with revenues under a million dollar—the mom and pops and individual entrepreneurs. And there are a lot of resources for companies that make a half-billion and above. But the companies in between, the $10 million to $250 million businesses, seem to get lost in the shuffle.

Business owners of mid-size companies can suffer from "The Founder's Syndrome"; they feel like the organizations they've created can't survive without them. This can erode both corporate growth and personal fulfillment. That's why I insist that my programs are custom-designed through what I call The FUEL Process. Through my process, I help business leaders find and utilize resources to engage teams and lead them toward their vision. I want mid-sized firms to benefit from the big consulting experience without the big consulting price tag.

I believe the $10 million to $250 million companies are the backbone of America, the world even. Think about small businesses, industry, and job creation. Visit any industrial park with office buildings—how many companies exist in those buildings that employ 10, 15, or 200 people? It's these companies that make or break our economy. It's not just about the P&Gs, Microsofts, and GEs. They're important, but they're not too big to fail. That's what entrepreneurship, small business leadership, and mid-sized companies are all about, and that's why I'm so passionate about them.

ABOUT THE AUTHOR

Mary Hladio is the founder of Ember Carriers Leadership Group, an organizational performance consulting firm that provides customized approaches to achieving greater levels of corporate efficiency, productivity, and satisfaction.

A specialist in organizational culture, team dynamics, and leadership effectiveness, Mary brings twenty years of experience to her engagements. She created The FUEL Process to help business leaders find and utilize resources to engage teams and lead them toward their vision. She also introduced the concept of "The Founder's Syndrome" to help business owners facilitate corporate growth and achieve personal fulfillment. Mary is also a licensed Insights Discovery® practitioner facilitating sessions in North America and Europe.

To learn more about Mary, visit her website at www.embercarriers.com.

facebook.com/EmberCarriers

twitter.com/EmberCarriers

www.linkedin.com/in/mhladio/

SEVENTEEN YEARS, TWO JOBS, AND A SONG

by Jason Yana

'''ve always seen things differently than most people. I don't just want to know how things work, I need to know. When I was a kid, I "borrowed" my dad's tools and dismantled the toy, game, or device within my reach. The ripple effect of parental consequences of this was two-fold. First, I destroyed a lot of things in our house trying to take them apart, conveying a lack of respect for my belongings. Second, I failed to return the screwdrivers to their proper location, showing a similar lack of concern about my father's tools.

From this wanton lack of appreciation for my things, I developed an affinity for design. I've always found beauty in functional objects, no matter how mundane. If you remove or change one little aspect of a part, it either doesn't work anymore or it's not as efficient. I eventually did learn how to put things back together without ruining them and actually developed an ability to fix things along the way. What I learned later, and built my own business on, is that knowing how things work is useless unless you can pass that information on to others in a dynamic and exciting way.

Fast forward to Architecture School. I quickly realized that not many people saw things quite the same way. I have always wanted to see and understand how every little connector, part, and component go together. While most students were interested in the outward appearance of the finished project, I was equally interested in all the elements you don't see once a building is completed. They are as beautiful to me as any stainless steel appliance, granite countertop, or other decorative design element.

After graduation, I took one last drive around campus, listening to The Cure's "Pictures of You," and feeling the weight of leaving all my dear friends and college life behind me. At this point I figured I would find a job at a big architectural firm in my hometown of Chicago and have a typical architectural career. It didn't happen that way at all....

I graduated from Miami University in Oxford, Ohio in 1995 with a degree in architecture. The job market was not good, but I had two offers on the table. One was from a giant firm in downtown Chicago which specialized in designing prisons. Romantic visions of designing the next great prison cell in a four foot wide cubicle in a windowless room danced in my head, yet I graciously declined that lucrative position. After foregoing what would certainly have been my fate as the next supermax designer of the year, I answered a "help wanted" ad in the local newspaper.

The interview was with Chuck, the Executive Director of a Masonry Trade Association which promotes the use of masonry construction materials in the Chicago area. Chuck was full of energy and passionate about my favorite construction material: brick. His fiery type A personality jived well with my keen attention to detail, and we spent seventeen years working together. I learned about marketing, engineering, architecture, and sales from Chuck. He gave me the latitude to do my job in any way I felt necessary, and I created the first masonry construction web site in 1997, which generated over a million users worldwide. My combined interests in what make things work, what make people tick, and my desire to leave things looking and working a little better than they were when I found them were all satisfied by this job for many years, but I eventually started to feel the call to something greater.

Words cannot describe my former boss and mentor's larger than life personality, so I will not try, other than to say that it was a pleasure working with him right up until the end. His sudden and unexpected retirement left me in a difficult position. It was like the floor I had been firmly standing on for seventeen years gave way underneath my feet and I was falling fast, so I decided to walk away. I put in my two weeks' notice and cleaned out my desk, leaving the security and safety of a regular nine to five gig. I walked out of there with two small boxes of personal items and I cued up "Pictures of You" for the first time since I left college with nothing but dreams ahead of me.

I drove away from seventeen years of dedicating my heart and soul to making the masonry industry better in any way I could. I was proud of the work I had done there. The tears welled up once again, followed by panic and fear of the unknown. As I listened to the song, that same feeling I had when I left college came over me—excitement about the unknown adventure that awaited. I still had plenty of dreams for my life, and this was my chance to start my own business, something my wife and daughter could really be proud of.

Here's one advantage of not being able to say no. For the last fifteen years, I had been running a side business, combining my two passions: architecture and 3D graphics. Over the years, companies took notice of my work and after about ten years of doing this, I had built a real income, all through word of mouth. When people asked me to do work for them, I couldn't say no because I loved it. I always knew that someday I would do this full-time and be my own boss. I had the boat fueled up next to the shore ready to depart for years, but for some reason, my boss' retirement gave me the push I needed to take the plunge and start my own business.

I went out on my own and started Jason Yana Studios (jasonyana. com). It's only been six months, but it has been the best six months of my professional life, and I will never work for anyone else ever again. It has been challenging and while it has not been very long, my business is thriving and things can only get better from here.

I plan to have only two "jobs" in my life. By the way, my first job was as a teenager working for Blockbuster, in case you were wondering.

What I realized along the way was that I love learning my clients' culture, discovering what matters to them, and meeting their needs. I recently went out of town to meet with the owners of a company I have worked with for several years and the hello was not a handshake, it was a hug from him and a hug and a kiss on the cheek from her. On the way home I thought about that moment and realized that it best explains what I do. Sure, I create 3D drawings of their products, but what I really do is work as hard as I can to ensure their success, the same way I would for a family member or good friend. So for all practical purposes, my answer to the question, "So, what do you do?" is simply, "I help my friends."

ABOUT THE AUTHOR

Jason Yana is an entrepreneur and the leading expert in visual building product marketing. His company, Jason Yana Studios, helps building product companies market and support their lines. He holds a degree in architecture from Miami University in Oxford Ohio and has two decades of experience in architectural technology, building product marketing, and 3D graphics. His innovative combination of architectural knowledge, 3D graphics, and animation skills have made him a sought-after consultant by many leading industry companies. To learn more about Jason, his services, and his insights on the visual demonstration of products, visit www.jasonyana.com.

www.facebook.com/JasonYanaStudios
twitter.com/jasonyanastudio
www.linkedin.com/in/jasonyana

THE "WHY"

by Kent Maerki

My name is Kent Maerki. I am the President and Founder of the Dental Support Plus Franchise and the ACE Financial Network. I am in a reflective mood, because my 71st birthday is just around the corner and I believe I only have twenty-nine more productive years ahead of me.

WOW, seventy-one, it's hard to imagine. I'm pretty sure I was only fifty just yesterday and only thirty-five a few weeks before that. Time goes by quickly when you're working on dynamic projects with dedicated, productive people. Looking back, I'd say I've always been blessed in that way. In my fifty-one years in business, I've had incredible opportunities to help people improve the quality of their lives and their balance sheets.

I've been an investment banker for over half of my life. I have raised more than $3 billion dollars in multiple industries, laying the foundations and implementing concepts for companies that have employed thousands of people and put billions back into our incredible economy. And even at age seventy-one, I'm still an active entrepreneur. I average over ninety hours per week educating and helping industrialists like you. We are the PRODUCERS of the world, and the world needs more of us! (If you're interested in learning about the real differences between "producers and looters," you may want to read one of my favorite books, *Atlas Shrugged*, by Ayn Rand.)

When people ask me what I do, I usually respond with, "Before I tell you "what" I do, I'd like to tell you "WHY" I do it." This approach is a game changer; it instantly draws and magnetizes the right people, including the press, and gets them excited about my business after they realize that they believe what I believe. The "WHY" concept was made famous by Simon Sinek in a "Ted Talk" titled, "How Great Leaders Inspire Action." I strongly suggest you watch it.

When you get the "WHY" right, everything else is easy.

Remember the Steven King book, *The Shinning*, and the subsequent movie starring Jack Nicholson? The book and the movie were based on the Stanley Hotel in Estes Park, Colorado, a famous grand hotel built by the inventor of the Stanley Steamer automobile. After a friend of mine bought it, we decided to preserve it. It took three years to have it listed as a Historic Property on the National Registry of Historic Places with National Significance. During that time, we produced award-winning plays there and received numerous awards. Our cast members ended up on TV shows. The "WHY"—it was a great hotel and should be saved.

In 1969 I built the fourth largest insurance agency in the country based on this "WHY": Help millions of people improve their financial conditions and get higher returns on their money while still saving a significant amount on insurance premiums.

In 1981, I was introduced to a new technology that could preserve food in transit. I'm not talking about adding a few days to the life of fruits, vegetables, flowers, and meat; I'm talking about weeks and months. At that time, about 15% of transported foods perished between harvest and market. Coincidentally, that 15% could solve the world food shortage problem and eliminate hunger. That became our mission; that became our "WHY." When people understood our why and what we believed in, they invested more than $1 billion dollars within thirty months. A chance to solve the world food shortage problem—why not? It was magical!

In the early 1980s, I was introduced to cellular phones. No one knew what they were. The engineer who built the first U.S. manufacturing plant took me to Washington, DC and showed me the future of telecommunications. I rode around Washington in a car with a curly antenna and equipment in the trunk while having a casual conversation with my mother in Chicago. I saw the future and held it in my hand. However, there were no cellular towers, no infrastructure, except in Washington and Finland. No one knew about it, and the ones who knew weren't paying attention.

We read the rules and found out that almost any US citizen was eligible to own cellular spectrum. We created The Cellular Corporation so the "little guys" would have an opportunity to get involved in this new technology. That was our "WHY." Everyone, not just the fat cats, deserved a chance to profit from this new industry called cellular radio telecommunication technology.

Because of our "WHY," people invested $75 million in nine months. Today the valuation of that cellular spectrum is worth over $3 billion dollars. What most people don't know is that the opportunity for anyone to own and control cellular spectrum still exists today.

I'm currently in the middle of the most important "WHY" of my life. Here it is…because of one missing piece of financial information, millions of Americans are about to fall over a financial cliff that will leave our young people shackled to the heavy burden of student loan debt for the rest of their lives and baby boomers and the elderly will be too frail to work yet too poor to retire. Maybe it's because I'm seventy-one and I see so many of my retired friends struggling or because I'm so darn mad at the looters (oops, I meant politicians) in Washington that this "WHY" keeps me working twelve or more hours each day.

After fifty years in the financial services industry, my opinion is that 95% of what we've have been taught about money and acquiring lifetime financial security is nonsense in today's economy. But there's good news too. In today's fast paced environment, it is easy to find investments and businesses that can generate "spendable cash flow" and long-term wealth.

But two things drive me crazy. First, the lack of practical business education. People don't know they can get the same monthly spendable profits from a simple $30,000 investment in an absentee owned and managed small business that they can from a traditional $400,000 investment in a CD or other traditional investments. Second, people don't know where to find these kind of businesses and investments.

The world is overrun with banks, brokers, and insurance companies that only offer their companies' approved products, which makes it extremely hard for the average investor to cut through all the smoke and greed-based advice out there. To solve these two issues I started an education based financial network. We call it the ACE Financial Network. A.C.E.S. assets include Automated Operations, Cash Flow, Equity Building, and Systems. They are the perfect complement to any recovery, retirement, or investment strategy. With these four foundational elements, business:

- Have Automated operations,
- Generate spendable Cash flow,
- Build Equity and value on a continual basis, and
- Maintain and improve through implementing rock solid, proven business Systems.

With our simple A.C.E.S. checklist system, I can teach anyone, from a sixteen-year-old student to a ninety-six-year-old retiree, how to evaluate almost any business and determine how they can meet their goals in ten minutes or less. It's the best thing I've ever done. If you or someone you know would like to learn more about A.C.E.S., I encourage you to visit our website at www.acefinancialnetwork.com.

ABOUT THE AUTHOR

 **Kent Maerki** was trained as an accountant and has been an investment banker for over forty years. He is the CEO and founder of ACE Financial Network and Dental Support Plus Franchise, one of the fastest growing franchises in America, with over six hundred units brought to market in less than thirty months. He was the founder of the Cellular Corporation, which gave small investors the opportunity to control cellular spectrum. Kent also franchised Super Shuttle (the blue vans you see at the airport), and created the IRA Institute, which helps individuals get higher returns from their IRA's and 401(k)s. His favorite book is *Atlas Shrugged*, by Ayn Rand.

To find out more about Kent, visit his website at: www. acefinancialnetwork.com.

www.linkedin.com/profile/view?id=6276048

www.facebook.com/kentmaerki

PLAYING JAZZ
WITH THE MASTERS

by Michael Ogorek

I hardly ever remember my dreams, but one night a vivid image from my subconscious was telling me something was seriously wrong. I jumped out of bed in a panic—my dream was screaming at me and would not be ignored.

I was fresh out of college, seven or eight months into my first professional gig working the graveyard shift on the police beat at a daily newspaper in a small town which felt like the other side of the world. I started out filled with excitement and anticipation about my new career, but found myself in a soul-sucking job in a dying town. Oops. Big mistake.

And then the dream. I was driving to work, entering the on-ramp of the freeway, wary of the cops who I had reported on. The signs were everywhere, what seemed to be dozens of them, bigger than life and screaming: "Wrong Way, Do Not Enter." It was only a dream, but I left that job soon afterwards. I began a lifelong search for something better; work that was meaningful and that would allow me to do what I loved with people I enjoyed working with. I told myself that I was in the middle of one of those learning experiences in which we end up learning as much or more from our mistakes and bad decisions than the things we do right.

Fast-forward a couple of years. After freelancing for several local publications, I started writing for a fledgling Detroit-area music magazine. It was a kitchen-table start-up that, to me, seemed full of promise. I was a relatively recent journalism school grad and played drums in a wedding band—it was perfect! At night I hung out with musicians, went to every jazz performance in town, and learned to listen with a whole new level of distinction. During the day I worked with writers, editors, photographers, and artists who all loved music. I was able to practice my craft and have fun creating a high-quality publication. I knew in my heart that we could take the magazine to the next level, so I borrowed money and became an investor. In my mind, I had made the leap from employee to owner. I had serious skin in the game and began to understand what it meant to be an entrepreneur. A shift was taking place inside of me. I started to dig deep and educate myself about sales and marketing and how to develop great products that consumers were willing to spend money on. I learned about building a team of people committed to achieving a shared vision and much, much more.

We gave it all we had, but in the end it just was not enough. The magazine went out of business, and I felt a profound sense of loss on many levels, but I knew something important had taken place and I would have done it all over again…hopefully not making the same mistakes, but I knew I would have made the same decision.

I started playing music again, abandoning my drum set and picking up the vibraphone, an instrument I fell in love with the first time I heard a recording by Milt Jackson. I was a newbie, but I booked gigs in local venues and surrounded myself with awesome talent, some of the best of the best Detroit-area jazz musicians. What a learning experience! My passion for playing music was re-ignited and while I don't play as often as I used to, music and what I have learned listening and playing is never far from the surface. I find myself applying the fundamental truths of music to everything I do. What is the most satisfying—and ultimately the most effective—is playing from the heart, creating something that has meaning, using your strengths, being aware of what's happening around you, and establishing a deep connection with your audience. In fact, every day I use jazz as a metaphor for the work I do with my clients, especially when employing strategy, creativity, innovation, and communication to reach the audience.

I went to work for a fast-growing company in the IT industry and started an entirely new chapter in my life. I found I had a knack for business development, strategy, marketing, and planning. I worked with talented business leaders and outstanding computer engineers. I worked with virtual global teams, defining projects for customers in multiple industries. Twenty years later I had gained an incredible breadth and depth of experience. One of my favorite projects was heading a new program dubbed the "idea incubator." My team and I generated innovative ideas to support our customer's marketing efforts. We developed an approach for creating new product concepts and quickly prototyping them. The work we did laid the groundwork for what I do today: develop innovative concepts, cultivate lean start-ups, and market new products and services.

But once again, that old feeling crept in again. While the signs weren't exactly saying "Wrong Way," I felt like I needed to return to entrepreneurship. I left the corporate world, started a real estate investment business, and took the roller coaster up and then down again. Yep, it was the recession and I was flat out overextended when the market turned. During this time, people started asking for my input about their business strategies. I consulted with a few local clients and realized that a lifetime of experience had prepared me to help these companies. While the tools and techniques have changed with the emergence of the Internet, social media, and online video marketing, the basic problems businesses and organizations face are surprising similar to those of the fledgling music magazine and my corporate IT clients. Marketing and innovation are critical; creativity and acting on inspiration are essential.

Today, I draw from all of my experiences: my early entrepreneurial challenges and successes, my corporate IT career, real estate investment successes and failures, and playing music. No matter what I am doing, I use the same collaborative, creative, and fun approach I use when I am playing jazz. I love finding innovative solutions that will help my clients become creators and innovators themselves. I love collaborating with clients to generate new ideas that bring value to their customers. I love helping them become authorities in their respective markets. I love being the catalyst for change and the instigator of success. When it's right, it's like playing jazz with the masters.

ABOUT THE AUTHOR

Whether it's creating a clear and compelling vision, developing effective business and marketing strategies, or implementing powerful Internet-based tactics, **Mike Ogorek** helps businesses attract and keep customers. Mike sorts through the confusion and designs roadmaps that enable businesses to connect and communicate with their customers in ways that establish trust and build connections that significantly impact the bottom line.

As a business owner, entrepreneur, and 20-year veteran of the IT industry, Mike has a proven track record of success in strategy and market planning, innovation, business development, and client delivery. In his spare time, Mike plays jazz on the vibes.

To learn more about Mike, visit his website at:

ogorekonline.com

www.facebook.com/OgorekOnline

twitter.com/OgorekOnline

www.linkedin.com/company/ogorek-online

HABITUAL SUCCESS

by Dwan Sullivan

M y divorce wiped me out financially. I was forced to downsize to a small, one bedroom apartment, and I knew then that I was done with women. I never wanted to get married again. Or so I thought.

At that time I was working as a train mechanic in Illinois. The winters were long, hard, and bitter cold. I would spend the day in the freezing snow and sleet mixed with the filth that builds up on the trains. The bosses who rotated in an out were modern day slave drivers, making life harder than it had be.

I felt trapped. I needed the benefits for my kids and the steady income to pay the rent; I just couldn't see a viable way out. Then I met the woman of my dreams (and yes, I married her). I felt as though she was an angel sent from Heaven. She introduced me to new ways of thinking and self-help and financial freedom books. Every spare moment I had was spent reading including my lunch breaks and late into the night. All this new information started to open my eyes to the possibilities of a better way of living. It started to ignite dreams I had put away long ago and I felt a sense of renewal.

I was still working as a train mechanic and my body was deteriorating from the years of hard physical labor. The sharp pain in my back started to shoot down my legs and left me nearly paralyzed if I twisted wrong or lifted something heavy. I started visiting a chiropractor and he told me I had a herniated disk, started me on therapy, and gave me nerve-deadening pills, but nothing seemed to help. One day the pain was so excruciating that I drove myself, very slowly, to the hospital where I was diagnosed with sciatica. I was put on disability for three months. I woke up one morning with a powerful realization that I was enslaved by my material possessions and my job. My time off enabled me to think more clearly and I knew I had to find a better way to live my life. I was determined to make a positive change and dump my job. I had been experimenting with different on and off-line money making plans, like MLMs, but none of them worked for me. I knew my health was in jeopardy and I needed to find something.

I talked it over with my wife and she said, "Let's get out of here." And that's exactly what we did. We packed up our bags and I dumped my job. We moved to Georgia and made the commitment to live beneath our means by minimizing and simplifying our life. We did a variety of little things such as consolidating our cell phones, using my employee discounts, and switching from an expensive bundled media bill to a MagicJack phone, Netflix, and basic Internet. We kept our thermostat at a lower temperature and wore an extra layer in the winter. We also learned how to use coupons in coordination with sales and pre-made our meals five days in advance, which saved both time and money. I had a part-time job and because we consolidated, we paid off both our cars within six months and saved enough to put a large down payment on a house, which made our monthly payment extremely low.

As a result of all of this, I had an abundance of free time. I was able to visit friends and family across the country whom I hadn't seen in years. I was able to attend marketing events and make new friends while learning how to grow as a person and launch a coaching business.

The possibilities began to open up for me. I felt like someone had taken the gauze off my damaged eyes, and I could finally see a clear path to financial freedom.

Today I help and empower others to live a life of freedom. I teach others how to change their financial habits so they can live a successful and abundant life. The trick is to take action and move forward. This can be difficult, but with the right tools and new habits, anything is possible.

What does wealth mean to you? It can be different for many people. For most, it means millions of dollars in the bank and a life of luxury. To me, the greatest wealth is the abundance of time. Time to do what you want to do with your life. Want to know how I continue to create a wealth of time to do what I want? I'll tell you, but only if you promise to use it to create your own abundance of time. The secret is to create it through habits. Let me show you how.

1. **Goals and milestones:** Write down your top three goals. Next, set milestones for achieving your first goal. A milestone is a 20–30 minute action you can take each day towards completing your goal. These simple actions will get you into the habit of setting and accomplishing more goals and milestones.

2. **Stop trying to be perfect:** Many people wait until they have the perfect idea before they take action, whether it is writing a book, delivering a speech, or even posting a video on their website. Don't let perfectionism stop you from implementing your projects. You can always make improvements and tweak as you go. Remember, nobody's perfect.

3. **Watch your words:** Up to 95% of what you say will dictate your mood. If you speak negatively then you will be less productive. If you speak positively then you will create positive emotions and excel in your undertakings.

4. **Motivation and commitment**: When we start a new idea or endeavor that is important to us, our emotions tend to run high and we are compelled to take off running with our project.

However, emotions can fade so make a commitment to yourself to keep going.

5. **Don't live beyond your means**: Don't spend more than you have. Be patient and live below your means. When you do this, you speed up the process to getting what you want out of life.

6. **Change your mental environment**: People with wealth have financial longevity because they are constantly learning. Read books, listen to audio programs, watch videos, meet with like-minded people, and find a mentor. (Here's a secret, your **income habits** work the same way.)

7. **Take educated action**: Knowledge becomes power when you apply it. As soon as you acquire the knowledge you need, act on it right away.

8. **Offer quality products and services**: Never offer products or services you would not use yourself. To create a life of income longevity you must first start with trust and authenticity.

9. **Market your passion**: Your product or service should provide a solution, solve a problem, or empower people. People take action to gain pleasure or avoid pain. Once you solve someone's problems, encourage him or her to tell others how you helped them and share that product or service with others.

10. **Share with people**: Earlier I mentioned finding a mentor. You should also take the time to mentor someone else. This will help you master the knowledge you have learned. Share for the sake of sharing. You could share a funny story, an amazing picture, or just some of your time. This is one of the most powerful life fulfilling things you can do for someone.

To your success!

ABOUT THE AUTHOR

 **Dwan Sullivan** leverages his expertise as an Internet marketer to help individuals retire in four years or less. As the author of the book, *Income Habits: Learn Habits to Retire in Four Years or Less*, Dwan empowers individuals to dump their job and create passive income. His techniques include on-line and other tailored strategies that build on passion and interests. To realize your financial freedom, visit <u>IncomeHabits.com</u>.

facebook.com/dwan.sullivan

twitter.com/sullivandwan

www.linkedin.com/pub/dwan-sullivan/4b/636/41b

I'M NOT A CRANKY YOGA MOM

by Kathleen Kizirnis

The real question is, what do I NOT do? I say this without the usual working-mother bitterness. Really. Like every other mother in the universe, I do a lot. Every day. What I don't do is make plans. I prepare dinner, do laundry, go to work, and pretty much everything else on the fly and, ideally, *in the flow*. It works, for the most part. As John Lennon said, "Life is what happens when you're busy making other plans." And who's cooler than John Lennon? (No one, in case you're wondering.)

When I finally stumbled into a "real" career at a newspaper after college, an editor asked me that exasperating, "Where do you see yourself in five years?" interview question. With a straight face, I replied, "Hell if I know." Surprisingly, I got the job. The following Monday I walked into the giant newsroom for the first time and was immediately thrown my first task: Rewrite an article in five minutes. Yes, FIVE minutes! I scrambled to complete it and send it off. There was no time for stalling when press time is mere hours away. In the newsroom, you either go with the flow or you sink. This job was perfect! I worked the copy desk, where you never know what's coming down the pike until it hits your desk. Maybe ten headlines in as many minutes. I learned to do what I could in the time I was allowed and to send it off just as fast, whether it was my best work or not even close. No rumination, no regrets, no time for fear—on to the next story and the next edition.

For years, cynicism was practically my middle name, along with skepticism, control freak, and, oh yes, selfish asshole. Then came (duh, duh, DUH) … "The Baby." My husband and I had planned, hoped, and dreamed for her. It was love at first sight.

Then reality struck as we quickly discovered she didn't like to sleep and rejected almost every bottle. We were exhausted. There was little room for selfishness, cynicism, or brain function. Ten pounds of cute and 2,000 decibels of utter, urgent need, that girl could decimate a week's worth of planning (as if) with one well-timed crying fit.

As much as I resisted the change, this new "flow" was a raging torrent. I was practically helpless and had no idea this Niagara Falls of a child was carving me into an entirely new shape (even after I got back into the pre-baby jeans). She moved mountains. I was on the verge of a breakdown. I knew something had to give. Between the stress at work and home, my sanity was at stake. I started taking a kickboxing class to burn calories and channel my stress. I also started taking yoga for stretching. A couple of classes later and I was hooked! The breathing, the calmness of it all, the incense! I found myself using the techniques in my daily life. It gave me the peace and serenity I had been yearning for. Cranky, smart-assed, over-caffeinated, cynical journalist met sweaty, heart-opening, incense-burning, green-juice-lovin' (still often coffee-buzzed) Yoga Mom. I had finally found my purpose!

After talking over my desire to become a yoga instructor with my husband, okay, more like pleading with him to let me do it, we agreed to put the wheels in motion. I began to learn all the different styles of yoga, from Vinyasa Yoga, Power Yoga, and Flow Yoga to Ashtanga, Anusara, Bikram, Kundalinia, and Yoga Booty Ballet. I learned very quickly how many styles of yoga there really are and dedicated myself to learning each one.

Fast-forward a few years. A sanity-saving hobby became a vibrant, growing, and immensely rewarding small business called Practice Yoga, in downtown Dayton, Ohio. It's all I do now; rather, it's IN all I do. In addition to teaching yoga, I write and teach to help clear up some of the misperceptions and help aspirants find the yoga that is right for them and maybe even the intuition they buried long ago.

Vinyasa (Sanskrit) means "movement with breath," or, "to place in a special way." Really, it means connecting with the moment—learning to respond instead of react. It's tapping into innate intelligence and intuition through goals and feedback, challenge and skill, focus and awareness, and timelessness and ease. It's so much more than physical. Series of poses are varied and, when intelligently sequenced, dance-like, even if your own physical grace is not so refined. Even if you can't touch your toes, you will bend, at least to some degree; you will flex muscle and stack bones, and you will sweat (at least in my classes).

I could go on and on. After almost a decade of study, I can't claim to know exactly how yoga works, and I don't need to. What I do know is that in this era of doing and achieving, of knowing our deadlines and lists better than we know our children, we need Vinyasa. Because somewhere in that joining of breath and movement, heart and limb, flesh and spirit (wherever you find it, on a yoga mat or elsewhere), we tap into a familiar knowing; a sense of peace and wholeness. Don't you think the world needs more of this?

As I tell my students (and anyone else who will listen), surrendering to flow, to what is, is not always pleasant. They feel it in their shaking quadriceps during a long Warrior pose or in a flood of emotion in a Corpse pose. Like the old news desk, in Vinyasa practice you never know what's coming down the pike until it does. You do what you can in the time you're allowed, and off it goes, whether it is your best, or not even close. Vinyasa is life training.

Do I still react in unhealthy ways? Heck, yeah, but not nearly as often. And I enjoy indulgences a lot more, thanks to my sharpened skills of awareness. I even like my kids more. What gets me out of bed and keeps me going to pricey trainings and teaching almost every day is connection, pure and simple. My passion is not so much the yoga itself as the bond that happens when a group comes together to, in a nutshell, get real.

In the words of one of my teachers, passion trumps everything … even mistakes, imperfections, misalignments, and missed deadlines. You have to trust it. Whether it's family or yoga or painting or, I don't know, selling fish, one thing holds true: When you dedicate your time to what you truly love and it feeds your spirit and somehow benefits others, you cannot fail.

It stops being about you and about something much bigger. Something urgent, demanding, growing, and dying. The plan gives way to a mission of spirit. That is Vinyasa. It is what connects and sustains us.

I bow to the light in you, and I hope it comes out blazing. Namaste.

ABOUT THE AUTHOR

Kathleen (Kathi) Kizirnis is co-founder and director of Practice Yoga in Dayton, Ohio; a vibrant, well-established school and community built on nothing but the passion for sharing yoga. She uses traditional yogic methods, including asana (postures), breath awareness, meditation, and more to awaken others to their own strength, purpose, and potential. Kathi believes that these empowering and healing practices belong to everyone and should be widely available and free of dogma for transformation on all levels—physical, mental, energetic, and spiritual. Kathi also writes about yoga and is a freelance editor. You can view her work at practiceyogadayton.com and upward-facingblog.blogspot.com.

facebook.com/practiceyogadayton
twitter.com/practiceyoga5th
www.linkedin.com/in/kathikizirnis

DIGGING FOR GOLD

by Rolanda Lang

t was time. I simply couldn't put one foot in front of the other anymore. Ever been there? It seemed crazy, especially with so many people out of work, to quit my job. But that's exactly what I did. I was making a great living working ten to twelve hour days, six days a week as a precious metals dealer, but I was exhausted, spent, mentally drained, and had absolutely no social life. Go out? Didn't have the energy. Work out? Please. On my one day off all I wanted to do was curl up in bed with a good book. My cohorts at work seemed to literally live out the motto, "always be closing." I just wanted to help people.

So during an economic crisis, which had cost so many people their jobs, I quit mine. Crazy, I know. However, I carefully planned my exit. I paid off all my debts and saved up some money, although I had no idea what I was going to do at the time. I just threw my hat over the proverbial fence knowing there was something better. There just had to be. And to be honest, I knew in my soul that the Spirit had something planned for me and I had to trust that.

Now, this is a far cry from the little girl who grew up to be an intense, focused workaholic who wouldn't settle for less than perfection, taking on the next challenge, hurdle, or hill with gusto to prove she was good enough. I grew up with an emotionally unavailable and verbally abusive stepfather who ruled the home with an iron fist. There was always a fear of doing something wrong, regardless of whether it actually was wrong. I learned very quickly to be resourceful, keep my head down, and get it right.

My stepfather and mother separated several times over the course of their thirteen-year marriage. During these separations, my mother received no financial support. She was a full-time wife and mother with little work experience and when they separated, she was left to raise two girls and make ends meet. In fact, during one separation, my mother took a job at an oil refinery and was injured on the job. She has chronic back pain to this day.

I was bounced from a nice upper-middle-class environment to a low-income environment several times. This lack of security instilled in me a strong desire to be independent and financially secure and I developed a workaholic type A personality with a wee bit of anal retentiveness thrown in to boot. Don't get me wrong, these are the traits that build successful careers, but success doesn't necessarily equate with fulfillment or happiness. I knew how to work; I didn't know how to live. Given my tumultuous childhood and various family dramas, my psyche took a beating. Even though I was financially successful and my stepfather was physically out of my life, he remained a constant presence in my head. I had developed a very strong critic: my own negative self-talk, which is kind of like an unwanted guest who doesn't know when it's time to leave.

Outwardly I looked and acted the part; inwardly, I was fraught with fear that I would screw something up. I knew my stuff, but my perception of self wouldn't allow me to believe it. In fact, I received hoards of glowing testimonials from clients and acknowledgements from management and even the president of the company. Goodness, what more could my inner critic want? When I finally learned to silence that inner critic, I was able to create a life I loved filled with work, joy, and balance. No more ten to twelve hour days for me.

When I was a little girl, I wanted to be a nurse, teacher, or police officer when I grew up. The common thread in these professions is service. I think because of my difficult childhood, I developed a desire to help people—to build them up versus tearing them down. Maybe it wasn't an accident that I chose the precious metals industry; it has given me the opportunity to help people protect their financial future against an uncertain economy. There have been countless times in my life when people have said I should be a coach. I was the go to person when friends needed to talk. Sometimes even strangers would just sit and spill their guts to me. I do enjoy teaching and absolutely love it when I can help someone reach their goals and accomplish their dreams. Ironic that I denied mine for so long because of that inner critic.

So, one day in the shower inspiration struck and I get this brilliant idea. Yep, I do my best thinking in the shower. Ping! A light went on. Ninety-nine percent of my former clients who invested in precious metals didn't know what to buy or even the right questions to ask. I had always consulted with my clients; however, most gold dealers only look at their bottom line, which is the commission on the sale. That day in the shower, I decided to start a consulting business in which I would represent and educate individuals who were looking to invest in precious metals AND write a "how to" book on investing in gold and silver. Yeah, yeah, there are other guides out there but they're all affiliated with gold and silver dealers, which is an inherent conflict of interest. So when this idea came bubbling forth, I knew I was on to something and didn't let that inner critic convince me otherwise. And for me, this was also a way of giving, teaching, and providing a valuable service.

I became an independent Buyer's Broker representing the interests of buyers investing in gold and silver with no affiliation or alliance to any broker. Seth Godin said, "Instead of wondering when your next vacation is, maybe you should set up a life you don't need to escape from." I desperately needed to escape from my life and welcome balance and joy back in. I'm here to tell you it's possible. I wake up every morning feeling happy and blessed. Remember, "Though no one can go back and make a brand new start, anyone can start from now and make a brand new ending" (Carl Bard).

If you're not happy with your lot in life, I encourage you to take a leap of faith and create a life that calls you forth every day. I don't necessarily recommend quitting your job like I did. Take small steps and don't forget to have fun during the process. Before you know it, you'll be there.

ABOUT THE AUTHOR

 **Rolanda Lang** worked for one of the top precious metals firms in Los Angeles and has eighteen years of experience in real estate, finance, and sales. She is an independent Buyer's Broker who represents individuals investing in gold and silver. She ensures her clients get the best price and value for their dollar by consulting with and negotiating the transaction for them. She has helped clients acquire $1500 to over one million dollars in precious metals.

If you are concerned about the state of the economy and want to protect your financial future, you can visit www.RolandaLang.com to learn more about Rolanda's services and download her e-book, *Industry Secrets on How to Properly Buy Gold and Silver—The Smart Investor's Guide.*

www.facebook.com/RolandaLang

SILVER LININGS

by Marshall Bone

W e are all familiar with the saying, "Every dark cloud contains a silver lining." Sometimes life's most catastrophic events can be the springboard to our calling in life. A few years ago, two such events shaped the path I travel today. It started with my dad passing away due to complications of Alzheimer's disease, and culminated in 2008 when my family lost our home due to my error. For two-and-a-half-years, my family drifted like nomads between the spare bedrooms of friends and family. A desire to learn how to protect my brain and make better decisions led to a study of brain science and quantum theory. My silver lining is that my experience allows me to help others grow the garden of their life out of the fertilizer of the past.

Each year, millions of well-intentioned men and women make resolutions to improve their lives. We commit to lose weight, get more organized, and stabilize our finances. Yet the next year we find ourselves making those same resolutions all over again. Don't feel alone, less than ten percent of people who make these types of commitments actually follow through with them. So is there something wrong with the rest of us? Are we doomed to live in the shadow of these super-achievers?

Before we proceed further, it is important that you understand something: There's nothing wrong with you. In fact, I have it on good authority that you were created with a spirit of power and love, with a calm well-balanced mind of discipline and self-control.[1] There really is no physical or mental difference between you and the super-achiever. So what explains the disconnect between what we want and what we have? It may surprise you to learn that your seeming lack of success is likely due to your body operating exactly as it was designed.

The body is an amazing masterpiece. For instance, nerve impulses travel to and from the brain at upwards of 170 miles per hour. It is like a non-stop NASCAR race in your body, except those impulses do more than just turn left. We truly are fearfully and wonderfully made! However, for the purpose of our discussion, the real star of the show is your brain. More to the point, understanding how to work with your brain is the key to success. The brain has three different sections. The reptilian brain handles things like breathing and reminding your heart to beat. On top of that is the midbrain, which contains your emotions. Finally, the cortex, where logic, creativity, and habit creation live. When you want to make a change, you need access to the cortex. Housed in your midbrain is an almond shaped structure called the amygdala, which controls your fight-or-flight response. Think of it as the gatekeeper for the cortex. Have you ever noticed that when you try to change a routine, that change is always met with a certain degree of fear? That is your amygdala in action. The fight-or-flight response is your friend when a tiger is chasing you, but what if all you want to do is create a positive new habit, can't it take the day off? Nope. It doesn't care if the trigger is a tiger, or a trip to the gym, if it is outside your standard routine, the amygdala leaps into action and shuts down the doorway to the all-important cortex. Can you begin to see why your resolutions are met with such resistance?

Fear not, there is a way to work with your brain instead of fighting against it. The answer is to think small. Which is more likely to sneak past a guard, an elephant or an ant? When you break your goals into small enough chunks, you slip past the amygdala and begin to create

_____

1   1: 2 Timothy 1:7 (AMP)

new neural pathways, otherwise known as habits. This flies in the face of the status quo, which tells us that the key is to take massive action. How's that working for you so far? We literally need to change our minds to bring our goals to fruition. Once we are thinking accurately, we can add some practical action steps, and just like a good recipe, the result will be delicious.

Most people live their lives in one of two places: the past or the future. They are either looking backwards, beating themselves up for past mistakes and missed opportunities, or anxiously looking forward into an uncertain future. Consider focusing on the present. I know, whenever you start talking about "being in the moment" it starts to sound mystical and super-spiritual, but nothing could be more practical.

The present moment is truly the only thing we have any real control over. Each day we have 1,440 freshly minted minutes deposited in our life. Are you going to spend them recklessly with nothing left to show for them at the end of the day, or will you invest them in activities that will yield a return in your future? Imagine making one small change each day that moves you in the direction of your goals. Nothing crazy, it could be as simple as doing one pushup or saying hi to one new person. These changes are small enough to slip past your fight-or-flight response, allowing you access to your cortex, which in turn will lead you to create new habits. If you build on those habits on a daily basis, they almost effortlessly become your new normal.

Allow me to share a personal example of how this works. At one point in my life I was terrified to talk to new people, but as a marketing professional, my living depended on developing new connections. My mentors would tell me to set massive goals like talking to 100 new people face-to-face every day. Can you guess the result of that misguided strategy? Not only did I fail miserably, I actually went backwards and retreated deeper into my comfort zone. Thanks a lot amygdala! Victory was eventually gained one person at a time. I simply started saying hi to one person a day, and as the fear dissipated I added one more person, then another. I started noticing that people seemed to appreciate my efforts to connect with them. My confidence soared! I upgraded and initiated conversations, easy things like asking for the time. Before I knew it, I was talking with twenty to thirty people a day. Instead of fighting my physiology, I learned how to work with it and bend it to my will. You can do the same thing.

Remember the process. A big goal leads to fear, which restricts access to the cortex, the area of the brain where habits are created, and eventually leads to failure. Breaking that goal down into small, bite-sized bits bypasses the fear, engages the cortex, and leads to success. Let me encourage you to keep one last thing in mind: Most people confuse facts with truth, but they are not always the same thing. For instance, today I am wearing a black shirt. This is a fact, but I can change that fact as quickly as I can change my shirt. Truth, however, is unchangeable. It may be a fact that up until this point you have failed to win in life, but with a little wisdom and the consistent application of some simple tools, that fact can change right now. When you learn to work with your body instead of against it, who you were yesterday does not have to be who you are today.

ABOUT THE AUTHOR

Marshall Bone is the co-founder and Chief Encouragement Officer of Bare Bones Media. A speaker, author, and online marketing consultant, Marshall's lifelong mission is to help people discover who they were created to be and give them the tools to pursue that calling. A native Californian, his wildly diverse interests include quantum physics, English Premier League football, and Duck Dynasty. He lives with his wife and son in Southern California. If you feel daring, you can read his blog at www.marshallbone.com.

facebook.com/marshall.bone
twitter.com/marshallbone
www.linkedin.com/marshallbone

ALL YOU NEED IS LOVE

by Mike McMahon

Have you ever had a moment in your life that literally changed everything? I have. I remember it like it was yesterday. My wife and I had signed up for a parenting class and we were sitting in the parking lot, anxious about attending our first session. I remember asking my wife, "What are we here for?" It wasn't like we had problems with our children.

We were busy people and both of us were already taking another class at the time. My wife, being the sensible one, said, "We're already here so why don't we at least check it out." We compromised. I agreed, but told her if the class wasn't life changing we were going to sneak out during the first break.

Twenty minutes into the class you could have picked my jaw up off the floor. The instructor introduced the idea that our kids actually transform our lives, not the other way around. This concept shook the very foundation of everything I believed about parenting. I quickly realized that everyone in my life contributed to my transformation: my children, my wife, my colleagues, and even my prospects. This revelation rocked my world.

At the time I was an extremely successful salesperson. I was well known amongst my peers as a master closer. Upon graduating high school, I got my insurance license and began selling right away. I attended the company training sessions and studied every sales book on the shelf. I knew the words of Tommy Hopkins, J. Douglas Edwards, Zig Ziglar, Brian Tracy, and Og Mandino like the back of my hand.

I love sales and selling, but for me it was a battle of wits or, as I used to call it, mental jousting. It was war, and I knew that learning how to make the perfect rebuttal and overcome any objection would generate more sales. I gave it my all and personally closed over 12,000 sales.

I've sold everything from businesses to Kirby vacuums. I've sold face-to-face, over the phone, inbound, outbound, long sales cycles, short sales cycles, big-ticket, and little ticket. You name it, I've done it. I became an expert closer, or as some people would say, a master manipulator.

I always believed that if I had the client's best interest in mind an aggressive approach was okay. It wasn't until the parenting class that I began to realize the truth and how wrong I had been. The class opened my eyes to what truly motivates people. All the sales guides I had read and training seminars I had attended taught me that pain is the greatest motivator. Tony Robbins, a well-known motivational speaker, talks about how people are either trying to gain pleasure or avoid pain, and that humans will work harder and do almost anything to avoid pain rather than to gain pleasure.

I lived by the pain and pleasure concept until it was pointed out in a parenting class of all things that the greatest motivator is love. I had to really think about that. I thought about the love a mother has for her child. Mothers will do anything to keep their children safe and care for them. I thought about the love I had for my wife and our children and what I would do to protect and provide for them.

The instructor of the class pointed out that God loved the world so much that He gave His only Son. This reminded me of my favorite sales book, *The Greatest Salesman In The World*, by Og Mandino. In chapter nine, Og says that the first principle to becoming the greatest salesman in the world is love. I'd read the book years before but I just didn't get it then. With a fresh perspective I reread the book, paying particular attention to chapter nine. Og's words and everything else I was learning changed my life and my sales strategy.

I knew that the old-school battlefield sales mentality was wrong, and that a new approach needed to be created. When you think about it, more has changed in the last ten years than in the previous century when it comes to how consumers are educated about products, companies, and the sales process. For the most part, sales and sales methods have remained the same. Companies are still using tactics and methodologies that our predecessors utilized 50 plus years ago; methods based on manipulation and pressure.

This was the beginning of my journey. I began to seek out experts in the sales industry who didn't rely on manipulation, aggressive closing, or overcoming objections. Needless to say, there weren't many out there.

So I asked myself, "What if there was a way to sell that didn't involve pressure, objections, or even the need to close?" What would it look like? What would have to change? How would you start? As I began working through these questions, I developed a process that accomplished exactly that.

The way to avoid pressure, objections, and the need to close is to simply stop selling. Imagine that! Instead of trying to sell someone a product or service, regardless of whether they actually need it (which is what I used to do), I developed a strategy to help people find solutions to real concerns. I discovered that by focusing on my clients' needs and presenting solutions to their problems, I received fewer objections and increased my sales. Hmm, maybe I was on to something.

If it's done right, closing is a natural byproduct of a compelling presentation. When the presentation is targeted toward a buyer's specific needs, as opposed to touting the product's features, it no longer produces objections and makes the solution seem obvious. The next step is writing up the order. In most cases, you won't even have to ask.

As I continued to test and refine the process, I became more and more successful. People bought and usually spent more. My customers began to give me more referrals and fewer returns. In fact, returns almost stopped completely. These days, I don't even teach salespeople how to close. If they are struggling to overcome objections or close they've something wrong.

All I had to do was treat people with respect and eliminate the pressure by letting them decide whether to buy based on their needs. I was no longer rejected and was stress-free for the first time. I was enjoying sales in a whole new and healthy way which motivated me to create "Healthy Selling," a system designed to transform the antiquated sales methods that everyone despises into a mutually beneficial process.

For many in the industry, it's hard to let go of the idea that you always need to be closing or overcoming objections. Prospecting can be fun, but healthy selling helps more people and helps you feel good about yourself.

ABOUT THE AUTHOR

Mike McMahon has personally closed more than 12,000 sales. After mastering, teaching, and utilizing every closing trick in the book, he created an innovative and modern sales approach based on the needs of the consumer.

In his groundbreaking new book, *Healthy Selling*, Mike criticizes what was once his bread and butter as "Battlefield Selling," a brutal, high-stress (for both salesperson and customer), and primitive system, and prescribes a new, fun, and civilized method that generates big results!

An insightful author, motivational speaker, and can-do consultant, Mike has a stellar track record of experience in executive sales, transforming and launching companies that have achieved over $145 million in sales.

To learn more about Mike or to receive a free report on selling without pressure, stress, or the need to close, visit: www. HealthySellingSystem.com.

facebook.com/healthyselling
facebook.com/healthyselling
www.linkedin.com/in/mdmcmahon/

FROM THE PROJECTS TO THE BOARDROOM

by Miguel A de Jesus

I grew up in an East Harlem neighborhood in New York City. When my parents became eligible, we moved from a small tenement housing area into public housing on the lower east side. We lived in a large apartment complex comprised of 16 buildings, 14 stories, and eight apartments per floor which all housed a family of three or more. This calculates to approximately 1,664 people residing in a small city block, or in other words, the projects.

Growing up surrounded by that many people and being exposed to diverse ethnicities, religions, and cultures helped me to learn how to be respectful, tolerant, and receptive to a variety of ideas and concepts. There were also many opportunities for my brother and I to fall in with the wrong crowd and follow a dangerous path of illegal activities, but we were lucky to be surrounded by a supportive family who taught us strong, traditional values and encouraged us to thrive in our environment. We also went to the local Boy's Club of New York and Boy's Brotherhood Republic facilities on a regular basis. These community centers offered a safe, friendly environment that engaged both our mental and physical energies through basketball, wrestling, boxing, table tennis, pool, and generally wholesome activities for kids who were determined to be "at risk"—we fell into that category.

I learned valuable life lessons growing up in the projects. I developed self-awareness, self-management, social awareness, and relationship management skills through my interactions and observations. Unfortunately, there was not much training or education available on these subjects, nor thought leaders capable or desirous of making a difference by communicating these new insights and personal development models to us at the time. Through my self-taught skills, I was able to objectively perceive my environment, and at a young age I knew I had to start making my way out of the projects.

I was able to attend (and graduate) from the High School of Music and Art, a special school for the musically gifted which was a two hour round trip commute through the NYC subway system. I subsequently enrolled at Long Island University, Brooklyn Campus. Upon graduating with a BS in political science, I chose to pursue an MBA at Columbia University. I left the MBA program before completing my final year and entered the business world because of one thing: money.

My need to earn money far outweighed the benefits of earning an advanced degree. It was time to recalibrate my goals and focus. I buried myself, knee deep, in the "business of business" by working for Xerox Corporation in a variety of leadership, results driven roles in both sales and operations for over nineteen years in four different markets. At the time, Xerox was a $15B Fortune 50 company.

After nearly twenty years I decided to shift gears. I have always been entrepreneurially driven and so I decided to take my skills and expertise to a smaller company. I joined the team at Paychex Inc., a $40M Rochester, NY based payroll and HR company at the time. My direction and leadership significantly contributed to the company's $2B growth. I held a variety of senior level executive positions, including VP of Sales for the Western US, in which I was responsible for the growth and development of 650 direct sales representatives, 130 First

Level Managers, and seven Senior Level Regional Sales Managers. My team consistently increased company revenue and market-share growth during my tenure with Paychex. They were a great group of people with a passion for winning and making a difference.

Throughout my life and career I've been curious, fascinated even, with the dynamics behind how people interact and treat each other. Why are certain people more likable than others? Why do some people manage to get more done? What makes people tick? I became driven to research the reasons why some leaders and individual contributors are more successful securing cooperation and support within their companies than others who seem to become de-railed by their inability to gain support and enthusiasm for their ideas and direction. It all comes down to this: People will work harder and produce more for those whom they know, like, trust, and respect.

This observation and principle applies everywhere—from the basketball court to the boardroom. Regardless of the environment, industry, or company size, it just works. In my quest and thirst to help businesses grow through strong management, I have learned, developed, honed in on, and discovered that the likability factor and the ability to influence stems from the core values and beliefs we hold.

I have nine core values and beliefs, which affect my thought processes and decisions:

1. Compassion: A deep awareness of and sympathy for another's suffering.
2. Helping Others: Help other people attain their goals and offer care and support.
3. Competence: Demonstrate a high degree of proficiency and knowledge through above average effectiveness and efficiency when completing tasks.
4. Achievement: A sense of accomplishment, mastery, and goal achievement.
5. Loyalty: Faithfulness, duty, dedication.

6. Knowledge: The pursuit of continual learning and development of skills and expertise.

7. Influence: Impacting or affecting the attitudes or opinions of other people: The power of persuasion.

8. Personal Development: Dedication to maximizing one's potential through self-development.

9. Seeking out and working with highly qualified coaches and mentors whose guidance significantly impacted the choices and decisions I made. The road to success was made easier through my associations with the right people at the right time.

Learning, studying, and applying these core values and decisions helped me become the successful businessman I am today. My experiences, the people I have met, and the entire journey have all shaped and molded me into the person I am.

My research also led me to my area of expertise: teaching others about Emotional Intelligence (EI) and how it can be more important than an IQ in the business and family setting. Studies have revealed that Emotional Intelligence has a significant impact on the success of school children and employees in different settings. This proves how superior EI is to an IQ. Or rather, how EI helps shape the IQ of a more holistic individual who excels at academe and performance leadership at work. I teach others about EI, what their EI is, and how it can change the way they interact with others to produce the desired results.

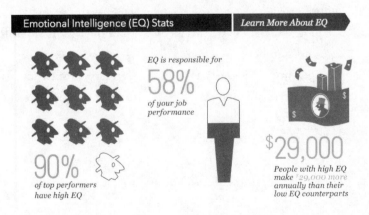

Emotional Intelligence (EQ) Stats — Learn More About EQ

EQ is responsible for 58% of your job performance

90% of top performers have high EQ

$29,000 People with high EQ make $29,000 more annually than their low EQ counterparts

ABOUT THE AUTHOR

Miguel de Jesus is the creator of the self-development website Discover Insider Secrets About Leadership, Getting Results, and Performance Management careerhelpsitemembers.com/get-started), which he created as a research and training community that helps those who want to improve and develop their leadership and social awareness skills.

A Keynote Resource speaker at Vistage International and EOS implementer, Miguel is also an Emotional Intelligence Certified Consultant as well as a Product Creation consultant with MakeMarketLaunchIT. He teaches Sales and Sales Leadership, Business Plan Development, and Product Creation and Distribution to executives, entrepreneurs, and individual contributors at his many speaking engagements.

Miguel resides in San Diego, CA and can be reached at miguel@coachmiguel.com.

facebook.com/askcoachmiguel
twitter.com/thecoachmiguel
www.linkedin.com/in/migueldj

AMPLIFY—15 STEPS TO LAUNCH FAST, GET TO CONTRACT & CASH CHECKS

Thomas K.R. Stovall

"**M**r. Stovall, please sign here…here…here, aaaaaand right here. Okay! We're all done! If you'll give me five minutes, I'll be back with copies of all the executed stock certificates for you." As Claire exits through one of the half dozen expansive glass doors that enclose one side of the conference room, I'm left sitting alone at a massive oak table. I gaze out the 18th floor window, and my mind wanders as a brisk spring day in downtown Chicago greets me. Six months ago, this business didn't exist and I had no income-not one dollar to my name. All I had was my Amplified Growth Plan. I sit here today, pen in hand, having just signed a deluge of documents authorizing my attorneys to release several million units of stock in my technology company to my initial investors.

I'm still not where I desire to be as it relates to career identity, business accomplishments or long-term financial stability, but the landscape of my life is very different than it was just 180 days ago. Within just six months of incorporation:

- Signed letters of commitment were secured from multi-billion dollar global companies and nationally recognized speakers to use my mobile business intelligence app, CANDID Cup, upon its launch.
- Over $100,000 was raised from private investors at a $3,000,000 valuation.
- A technology partnership worth over $500,000 was negotiated with an enterprise application development company for development of version 1 of CANDID Cup
- Version 1 of CANDID Cup was completed and approved in the Apple App store.
- Three highly seasoned and well-connected business development experts joined the team, including one who came in 3rd on season three of "The Apprentice."
- Within two weeks of being approved in the Apple store, CANDID Cup was named the official feedback app of a VIP online marketing and social media conference in downtown Chicago, which featured some of the top paid and most well known online marketing experts and technology entrepreneurs in the world.

I'm present to how surreal this moment is, and I begin to think back on how I got here...

By the age of thirty, I had raised close to $250,000 in private investment capital and amassed over $2.5MM in real estate holdings in my portfolio, having started with my entire savings of only $3000. My business grew faster than I was prepared for or knew how to manage. With no mentorship and no team, my rapidly expanding house of cards eventually crumbled. In the end I lost everything, including my $350,000 dream condo, which I had proudly purchased a few years earlier.

After closing my real estate investment firm in mid-2010, I had NOTHING. Credit ruined, no money in the bank, my name was now mud with my investors, and my confidence had taken a major hit. There was something I was missing.

On July 21st, 2010 I began participating in a scarcely known and highly specialized business philosophy and curriculum. I soon realized that I had finally found the secret formula to sustainable and systematic business growth that I had been searching for all those years. There ARE specific steps to take in a specific order that produce reliable, predictable results. After close to two-and-a-half years of intense study, practice and application of the principles in this curriculum, I found a way to combine what I had learned with my own business experience, unique pre-existing skill set, and personal process for building businesses. My $3MM mobile app and the entire business around it were built in 180 days using this process.

In my Amplified Growth methodology, there are six stages and thirty-five specific sub-categories of business growth and development that a company must move through in order to build a scalable structure, focus its time and resources, and create exponential growth. Below you will find a practical fifteen step outline that gives you the cliff notes overview of my process. If you follow these steps in order, you WILL amplify the growth of your business and produce explosive results.

Step 1 :: Be Afraid, Do It Anyway

The fear NEVER goes away, just hit the go button. Total failure is a concept that doesn't really exist; there's only FAILURE TO MEET A GOAL that you set. That said, fail fast, dust yourself off, re-assess, do it again.

Step 2 :: Set Your Coordinates

Clearly articulate your vision and mission, because if you can't see it, you can't say it, and if you can't say it, you can't do it. You can't get to a specific spot on the grid if you don't know the coordinates.

Step 3 :: Create A Bullseye

Don't be a generalist. Create a niche and define your specific, ideal customer. It's counter intuitive, but the more specific you get, the easier it is to find them, and the easier it is for them to find you.

Step 4 :: Accurate Thinking

Vet the idea with experts and REAL PEOPLE immediately and have them poke as many holes in your balloon as possible, as quickly as possible, then make the adjustments.

Step 5 :: Remove Your Ego

Do you currently have the specialized knowledge, track record and skill set to stand up in front of ANY investor, customer or strategic partner and get their buy-in? If not, get over yourself and transact for the help of a specialist who does and get them on your team ASAP.

Step 6 :: Trusted, Vetted Relationships

Everything and everyone you need is already in your network or one degree away, you're just not asking. Money, specialized knowledge, talent, access; It's all there. Go deep inside your network and make powerful requests, you'll get results much faster because you're moving inside of trust.

Step 7 :: Be Geppetto

Self-employed mindsets try to be expert at everything and trust no one in their business. Business owner mindsets master identifying what's needed, then recruiting and effectively managing specialists in every area of the business who are smarter and more seasoned than themselves.

Step 8 :: Look the Part

Move with the knowledge that EVERYTHING you say, everything you do, everything you wear, everything you present, and everyone who is associated with your business are ALL a reflection of the perceived quality and viability of your business and your level of competence and ability in fulfilling on the mission as the owner.

Step 9 :: Gnat-Level Detail

Be painfully and annoyingly specific in your internal and external documents as you define your vision, mission, target, as well as your brand identity and narratives. Every word, every detail, every pixel matters. That doesn't mean perfection, it means precision.

Step 10 :: Show Me the Money

Clearly define how you'll make money. "Build it and they will come" is a fantasy, and at best, this type of thinking slows the pace of exponential growth potential. Define the actual strategy and objective numbers required to grow your business and close deals with your specific customer, by day, by week, by month, by year.

Step 11 :: Build Your Team on a Budget

If you don't have cash to pay people, barter, create strategic partnerships, call in favors, and leverage relationships to form your team initially. Start by creating a solid Advisory Board of highly seasoned business people who believe in and trust you. They will help you define and attract the additional team members you need.

Step 12 :: Documentation

NOTHING exists outside of the four corners of a contract. Do NOT move in the world of "good intentions." Have everyone associated with your business sign confidentiality agreements and contracts for everything. No gray space, clear expectations.

Step 13 :: Time…Friend or Foe?

Time is of the essence, and every single second that goes by after the launch of your business is either building your track record, or diminishing it. Stay in stealth until you go live, but once you officially launch, you had better be ready to pull the trigger.

Step 14 :: Master the Invitation

Whether you know it or not, the single most effective tool in rapidly building a business is creating tremendous first impressions. A masterful and compelling invitation closes the deal and secures the buy-in of strategic partners before you ever begin the presentation. Ponder how to be extraordinary in your approach.

Step 15 :: Make 'Em Smell You, Leave Your Scent Behind

Your collateral materials are everything. At a minimum, you need a power point with rich, visually engaging graphics and concrete facts, figures and case studies. Invest in a video and a website. If you can't afford a professional, go to the local college and find a top-notch student to do it. Present yourself and your business in ways that are so compelling and creative that you are forever imprinted on the memory of your prospects.

To view Steps 11-15 and get access to an in depth video series breaking down each of the 15 Steps in line item detail and how to implement them in your business, visit: www.NoExcuseBiz.com.

ABOUT THE AUTHOR

Thomas K.R. Stovall is an entrepreneur with over 14 years of business experience, specialized study and training in the areas of business amplification, project management, leadership development, sales, viral marketing, transformational learning and ontology. While attaining his bachelor's degree in Electrical Engineering at Tennessee State University, he started his first business selling luxury custom wheels and performance tires to online customers from California to New York out of his dorm room, and has been an entrepreneur ever since.

At a glance, Thomas' business experience includes private equity, real estate investment, large-scale event production, business amplification consulting, and more.

For more information, visit: www.LinkedIn.com/in/ThomasKRStovall

BLENDING MAGIC

by Nathan Schneider

C arrots in ice cream, cabbage in coffee, and a group of people thinking I'm crazy. Who would've thought recipes that sound so disgusting would result in comments such as "amazing," "life changing," and "I want that recipe"! I started my business because I thought I needed to make more money; today I realize what I really needed was nutrition.

I was a nineteen-year-old college student and about fifty cents short for one hard shell taco at Taco Bell. Thinking I had more loose change in my car than I did, I left hungry. I had moved out of my parents' house and was working two jobs to pay for my education and expenses. Not being able to afford one taco isn't something I wish to remember, or even share, but it was a landmark that ultimately led to my passion and what I do today.

Not only was I broke, I was unhealthy. My real problem was that I didn't know it because I never knew what it felt like to be healthy. I thought some people were simply born with a vast amount of energy. I thought people got migraines because of their genetic make-up. Physically, I was always tired and sick; mentally, I had a terrible memory, couldn't focus, and didn't do well in school. I thought I received the short end of the stick when it came to health, and I never considered nutrition as a contributing factor.

I realized two things at this point in my life: I was going to do whatever it took to live a life without such basic limitations and I was sick of Ramen noodles! I began my journey by studying successful people. I saved up enough money to fly across the U.S. to attend seminars hosted by motivational speakers like Les Brown and health guru Dr. OZ (before he had his first T.V. show) and bought books and audio tapes of business leaders such as Jim Rohn, Napolean Hill, and Stephen Covey. I soaked up as much information from them as I possibly could.

Although I too wanted to be successful, my poor memory and low energy level, among other problems, frustrated me. I thought, "What's the point if I forget what I learn and spend most of my money on energy drinks?" Then I heard this quote from Jim Rohn: "Some people don't do well simply because they don't feel well." Luckily, Jim didn't stop there. He emphasized the WHY and HOW of living a healthy life. This is when I first realized my health NEEDED to improve before I could do anything.

It wasn't long before I decided to study health and nutrition. It was a whole new world with contradicting books, studies, diets, and opinions. I started selling memberships at a gym and learned the diet and fitness perspectives of personal trainers. At the same time, I was hired to sell a new "healthy" energy drink at wholesale clubs—a product I enjoyed because it solved my energy problem. I will never forget the day I pitched that product to a Costco member: "Hey Miss, would you like to try a healthy energy…" Her immediate response was, "No, I don't need that fake energy, I have a Vitamix machine." I was confused and she was gone before I could respond. I was sure she misheard me.

There was a Vitamix demonstration at the same Costco and I quickly discovered that this machine made soup from scratch in minutes, whole fruit and vegetable smoothies and juices without extracting the pulp, and ice cream with natural ingredients. The machine held a two horsepower motor and could whip peanuts (and only peanuts) into creamy peanut butter in under a minute. It took less than 15 seconds to clean. Like many others, I was hooked! I found out the company was looking for help in the area, so I took a chance. I still remember my dad's comment after I told him I was going to work for Vitamix: "Vitamix? I think we have one of those." To which I responded, "No way Dad, I remember the one we had. Vitamix makes soup and even ice cream." But he was right; we did have one when I was growing up. I guess you really do go back to your roots.

During the next five years, I traveled across the Midwest demonstrating and selling Vitamix machines at wholesale clubs and state fairs. I heard an incredible amount of information and contradicting viewpoints about health and nutrition, most of which was unrelated to the machine and my job. For example, I've heard: "Milk is not meant for human consumption," "Milk is great for your bones," and "Milk does nothing for your bones." I was overwhelmed and confused and spent many nights searching for the truth.

I finally gained an understanding of what the body needs and was able to make changes. The headaches stopped. I developed a sharp memory. I no longer needed an energy drink to start my day. What that lady told me in Costco finally made sense. With help from the Vitamix machine, I improved my health and didn't need fake energy! I looked good but more importantly, I felt good. It wasn't genetics; it was the synthetic junk I was putting into my body.

I was a whole new person and health became my passion. I became addicted to helping others change their diets. I couldn't allow myself to just sell the machine; I got to know as many people as I could, shared information, and helped them develop strategies tailored to their goals. One of the first sales I made was to Dennis LaMott, from Apple Valley, MN. In his words: "I lost a total of 56 pounds from July to the end of January." All Dennis had to do was replace one meal a day using the Vitamix machine.

If Dennis and I can change, why can't others? We were not only in the right place at the right time, we both put our all into improving our health. Most people don't and the primary reason is because there are so many diverse viewpoints regarding what is healthy. With all the contradicting information out there, such as the milk example above, it's easy for anyone to become confused. Some try and fail, and some don't try at all. Like technology and social media, our understanding of food, nutrition, and health significantly differs today compared to decades ago and is continually changing. What was 100% true decades ago could possibly be false today. To help clarify this problem, I wrote a short e-book titled, *Health in a Nutshell*, which provides up-to-date, straightforward information.

I've been lucky enough to completely re-invent not only my health but my life. My goal is to inspire others to do the same. I demonstrate and sell Vitamix machines across the Midwest, create crazy great tasting recipes jam packed with veggies, and share them on my site www. BlendVersity.com.

ABOUT THE AUTHOR

Nathan Schneider is an entrepreneur, salesman, and Big Brother Big Sisters volunteer. With his expertise in health, blending, and sales, Nate has been the #1 Vitamix regional salesperson the past two years and turned his home state fair (Minnesota) into the top sales show in the U.S. He created www.BlendVersity. com and is the co-owner of www.UneekSites. com and the Del Sol-Color Change retail store in Branson, MO. Nate will debut his latest invention, a universal kitchen system tool, at the end of 2013.

As a bonus to all *So, What Do You Do?* readers, Nathan is personally giving away:

A free Vitamix machine to one lucky winner;

A free copy of his e-book, *Health in a Nutshell*; and

Three popular recipes (a delicious vegan ice-cream, lime-sorbet, and Frappuccino®) and three free tips to all current and future blender owners.

For details about how to claim these giveaways, visit <u>www. BlendVersity.com/sowhatdoyoudo</u>.

facebook.com/BlendVersity.com

twitter.com/N8Schneider

www.linkedin.com/in/n8schneider/

THE ROAD TO RECOVERY

by Peter Engert

As a physical therapist, I'm often recognized on the street by the patients I've treated. One day after work, I went to dinner at a restaurant near my North Side Chicago residence. I put my coat in the booth, went to the bathroom to wash my hands, and when I returned, there was a twenty-something-year-old girl sitting at my table. She called out, "Hi Peter, it's so good to see you. How are you?" I sat down and said, "Good, you?" with a quizzical look on my face. I was trying to recall how I knew this girl.

She asked me if I remembered her. I'm not really sure, I said, "Are you from Cook County Hospital?"

"No!"

"Oak Forest Hospital?"

"No!" She yelled, "No, don't you remember, I'm Latosha from Cook County Jail!" By now, everyone in the restaurant was staring, and I kind of slink down in my chair. "You were my physical therapist there," she said in a lower voice. "By the way do you have a girlfriend?"

Uh oh, I think. "Yes I do," I respond.

"Oh, I have this gold chain, maybe your girlfriend would like it. Here check it out. Maybe you want to buy it for her?" Relieved, I tell her I'm not interested and we chat for a few minutes more before the host comes over and politely asks her to leave. Upon leaving, she says, "Look Peter, I am walking normal again just like you taught me. Thank you."

I returned to eating my dinner and thought to myself, wow, here's a perfect example of an incarcerated patient I treated who didn't stay in jail. And because she received the proper care when she was there, she now has a chance to get her life back on track. My twenty-year career as a physical therapist, the first half in Cook County Hospital and part-time at Cook County Jail and the last half in home health care, has taught me that the mind and body connection is a powerful attribute that we are just beginning to understand. I have seen patients with little potential and a lot of drive succeed, and others with a lot of potential and little drive fail miserably. How the human body heals itself is an amazing process, and medical technology is slowly catching up with it.

I also believe we often give up on our recovery too soon. The main reason for this is that our benefits run out and we have no money to pay for the care we require. Consequently, we stop trying to continue to improve ourselves after a few short months. The first year is often the most critical time for recovery, but sometimes the body needs even more time and work, which is when most people give up. For example, I worked with a 91-year-old male patient who is bound to a wheelchair due to the weakness in his legs brought on by a stroke. When I initially evaluated him, he expressed a desire to walk again (which he had not done in the last year), but I was hesitant to even entertain that thought. My goal was to be able to transfer him in and out of the wheelchair with minimal assistance so he could stand and practice his balance in order to improve his ADLs and make it easier for the caregiver to assist him.

We practiced standing up while holding onto a bar in his facility's weight room, and we tried marching in place, which I figured would be impossible. But he was able to do it. I began to have some hope of progressing to a rolling walker, but I knew it wouldn't be easy. The patient is 6'4" and not the lightest person—it's difficult even for me to handle him without an overhead harness. But this patient was very determined. I showed him some exercises he could go through with his caregiver, which he practiced diligently when I wasn't there. After a few weeks we attempted to walk with the rolling walker, which was a struggle, and my back hurt for a couple days after trying to get him up. To make a long story short, after two months of physical therapy two times a week, my patient was able to walk about 100 feet with the rolling walker and assistance which, considering I didn't think he was going to walk at all, is pretty amazing. He is my "Miracle Walker." He proves my point that we often give up too soon in our recovery process.

Most people have no idea what physical therapist do, even other medical professionals aren't really sure what our role is. That's why I launched www.AwesomePhysicalTherapy.com. I want to educate the public about the many roles of physical therapists and how they can help their patients. I'm also currently working on a book to educate patients about home health care and what to expect. Having been a home health physical therapist for the last 10 years, I understand the overwhelming feeling that many patients and family members encounter. Often, when elderly parents and relatives return home from being treated in a hospital, they have many different problems that need to be addressed. They may not be able to live on their own anymore or if they do, require constant care. This is often a difficult thing for many patients to accept. I think the hardest thing about getting older is losing one's independence. My goal is to help minimize the difficulties that patients and families endure in the course of this transition.

ABOUT THE AUTHOR

 **Peter Engert, MPT** is an accomplished physical therapist with nineteen years of experience. After graduating from Skidmore College in New York with a BA in biology and English, he pursued a Master's in Physical Therapy at Northwestern University Medical School in Chicago, IL and was personally mentored by the Horatio Alger award-winning William E. Bailey.

Peter began his career at the infamous Cook County Hospital (now Stroger Hospital), and part-time, he ran the physical therapy department at Cermak Hospital located in Cook County Jail. Upon leaving County Hospital, Peter began working in the home health care field and continues to help patients progress on their road to recovery.

For five quick tips on home health care and other life changing information about physical therapy and how it can impact you and your family, visit www.AwesomePhysicalTherapy.com.

www.facebook.com/peter.j.engert

www.linkedin.com/profile/view?id=19440605

SURVIVING DOMESTIC ENSLAVEMENT

by Paula Thomas

I t all began in the 1960's when my parents joined a network marketing company that was the epitome of pyramid schemes. My dad's sales pitch was so convincing he could sell ice to Eskimos. He was a master!

My dad quit his teaching job at the local college and we moved from the comfortable home we had lived in for five years into a bigger house. My parents were making a considerable amount of money and then it all came tumbling down. My parents and younger sisters moved in the middle of the night, and I stayed to graduate from high school. The house was gone, the cars got repossessed, and our lives changed. I promised myself I would never do anything risky like that, but I suppose entrepreneurship is in my blood.

I met my second husband after a horrible divorce and custody battle over my daughter. I had also lost a daughter to a rare liver disease at thirteen months. My husband was my knight in shining armor. I knew deep down that something wasn't quite right but I chose to ignore my instincts and move forward. I saw in him the person he wanted to be and I kept working to help him get there.

Two years into our marriage, God moved my heart and I wanted to have another child. I gave birth to the most amazing son and life was great…and then my husband became more and more controlling. He went to work very early in the morning and I had to have his clothes ready and his shoes shined before he left. When he came home, dinner had to be on the table the moment he walked through the door and the children had to be spotless. Money was a huge issue for him and a "thing" hanging over my head. I was given a small allowance and he consistently reminded me that I would be nothing without him. At first he was not physically threatening, but his words were like daggers piercing my heart. He got a look on his face when he was angry that terrified me. From all appearances, we were the perfect family. We lived in an 8,000 square foot home, I was driving a Mercedes, and wore diamonds and designer clothing. I was putting on a good front and trying to keep everyone happy, but inside I was miserable.

In 1996, while working with my husband at his chiropractic clinic, I was introduced to a wonderful company and weight loss wellness product (Calorad) that would literally save and change my life. I loved it; it seemed like a good fit for our clinic and a way for me to earn a little money of my own. My husband was fine with this venture until he realized it was diverting my attention from him. I was getting results and having fun and the more successful I became, the angrier he got. It was at this point that I realized I was in bondage.

One night I was on the phone with a friend and she heard him confront me. She begged me to stay on the phone while she called the police. It was the beginning of the end. My daughter was in college and I could no longer raise my son in this environment. It was time to move on and for the first time in my marriage, I realized I wasn't worthless. I had the ability to sell and motivate other people and make it on my own. My EYI business was doing very well and now I was free to really build it. I earned six figures my first year, doubled it the second, and it kept growing. The best part was that I was able to be home with my son and attend all his school activities and athletic events. I loved entrepreneurship!

About five years in, ownership of the company switched hands and the compensation plan began to change. It changed four times before the company finally collapsed. I was devastated! I thought about what my parents went through and heard my husband's voice in my head telling me I was going to fail. But I knew in my heart I had the fight and motivation I needed to be successful—I just needed to find the right product.

I began looking for another company and tried a few, but my heart and passion were not in it and I couldn't sell something I did not completely believe in. It was about this time that I met my current husband. He has helped me in so many ways and supported my dreams from the beginning. He sees my potential and encourages me to achieve more!

I was still looking for a nutritional company and dabbling in the one I had recently joined when opportunity struck. My husband and I were boating and met a couple. We started talking and the woman told me she sold a line of jewelry for a national company called Silpada. After she showed me the product, I was sold on the spot. I told her I was a networker and wanted to sign up to purchase the jewelry at cost…BUT..I was not ready to become a rep, attend meetings, or build a business. She agreed and I picked out half of the items in the catalog.

The quality of the jewelry was so good and all my girlfriends wanted to buy it. It wasn't long before I signed up as a rep. I started getting information about our national conference; I knew if I was going to do anything with this business, I had to meet the owners and find out what they stood for. I was overwhelmed! I actually cried because I had never felt so appreciated and cared for before. They wanted the best for us and still do!

I am a recruiting maniac. You don't know what a person is going through and I wouldn't want to walk away from anyone who might be in a situation like I was. My passion is empowering women and I am going to make sure I do everything possible to help everyone I can achieve their dreams and become successful!

One of my favorite stories is about a single young mother of three. She worked full-time but didn't make enough to afford her own apartment, so she lived with her parents. She heard about Silpada and contacted me. She began her business and not only did she earn enough to move out, she gained enough confidence to apply for a higher paying job! Silpada gave her the extra boost she needed and the extra income made all the difference for her!

I have earned many national awards, and walked the stage many times. When they dangle a carrot in front of me, I am one of the first to achieve a goal. But the best part of my business is watching a new rep achieve her goals and gain self- confidence!

I love my business because there is no pressure. The quality of the jewelry sells itself and each piece has a lifetime guarantee. I say I love my "JOB," but I don't think of it as work. Silpada is a family of caring people who enjoy helping each other and have fun doing it!

ABOUT THE AUTHOR

Paula Thomas is a seasoned networker with over twenty years of experience as a speaker, and national trainer on many subjects—primarily building strong teams. Her personal growth and commitment to her business and team make her a sought after mentor. Paula's humor and personality will sell you, but her desire to empower others to reach their greatest potential will capture you! You can learn more about Paula and her business at www.mysilpada.com/paula.thomas.

www.linkedin.com/profile/view?id=188821951

www.facebook.com/paulasbling

THE GREATEST GIFT YOU CAN GIVE YOURSELF

by Kim Burger

Gifts come in many packages, so do people. Have you ever opened a very big package, full of excitement and wonder, only to find a very small token inside? This was always a fun trick with the kiddos when they were young. I have always felt like this beautiful tiny soul wrapped up in this huge package that really didn't fit ME!

Being a kid was the BEST! Remember when going to school was nothing more than a social event, walking home was always an adventure, you spent 15 minutes doing homework, and had plenty of daylight left to go play with your friends! You hand-wrote your homework because there were no PC's, your clothes actually got dirty from playing, and the biggest stress in life was waiting until your friends were done with dinner to play some more!

I was very young, nine years old to be exact, when my parents moved across town and not only was I ripped away from the only life I knew, I had to start a new school with kids I didn't know. I was popular at my old school because of my older brother and sisters. I was on the 6th grade cheerleading squad as a 3rd grader. You would think that my life would not be all that different 15 miles away…but it was. Everything changed.

That summer before 4th grade, I sat inside watching the old groove tube, eating more food than most adults! By the time I started school I had become the "Fat Kid." I knew that I was the same inside…but none of that mattered. New kids, new rules, and I was the one they picked on; not by all the kids, and not so bad that I cried myself to sleep every night, but it hurt nonetheless. I still managed to make the cheerleading team, as the lifter. I was the biggest girl on the squad, and I remember my mom altering my uniform and having to wear the "Husky Jeans" from Sears. It was bad enough they were for big kids, but they were for BOYS!

Fast forward to the summer before 8th grade. My aunt, being the most self-conscious person (in a good way) I know, took me in for several weeks and put me on my first diet. Yes, I call it a "diet" and a shake diet of all things! She taught me a lot of things that summer like how to count carbs, how to blow-dry and curl my hair just like Farrah Fawcett (so 70's), and even how to apply makeup. I swam everyday, which was great for the tan, rode bicycles which was great exercise and ate, or should I say did not eat! All the same, it was fun, and when I went back home it was like I was a new person, at least on the outside.

Life continued and at twenty-two I was married and became a mom. I had it all: the husband, the house, and my precious first-born son. I immediately went to Weight Watchers to get back into my pre-pregnancy clothes. By no means was I small, I just strived for comfortable. My husband at the time liked to cook, and I know not all the blame can be attributed to him because I liked to eat. My weight would fluctuate a good 80 lbs. easily. Then came baby #2 and again my weight went up and up. Funny thing how we treat our weight like money…some people are spenders (eaters), some are savers (conscientious), and some are in plain denial. All I knew is that I was miserable and something had to change. So I took the easy route and resolved to just love myself the way

I was. That didn't last long because as I reached the depths of despair and basically gave up, my husband had also reached his breaking point and compounded the problem by vocalizing his disappointment, teasing me, and finally withdrawing his love.

Again, I reached down and pulled up my BIG GIRL panties and lost yet another 80 lbs. Now at some point, even as a reader, you have to say "Stop the Madness"! When the cycle started once again and before it went too far, I looked deep inside myself and demanded a healthy relationship! That was the missing link. How we allow people to treat us and how we process that treatment can have a huge impact on our minds and bodies. Think of it as a game of poker—you can only change a few cards in the hand you are dealt. The rest is how you choose to stand, call, raise, or bluff. I chose to stand for what I believed in, mainly me, and teach myself to live in the body I was dealt and take care of it.

The decisions I made were tough. One of my dear friends would always tell me, "The right thing to do is always the hardest thing to do." I went out on my own, overcame many blocks, and have maintained a healthy weight zone since 2011. I have kept that ugly 80 lbs. off for more than thirteen years!

Today I am a Life Coach specializing in Mind and Body work, bridging the gaps that hold us back. Have you ever desperately wanted to lose weight but always had an excuse for putting it off? Have you ever wanted to look your best for an upcoming special event but ended up sabotaging yourself by putting on more weight? You know that you have! These are blocks that prevent the mind and body from working in unison and as a result, no change takes place. I teach people how to quickly and easily sync the two in order to make measurable progress.

I can see through the B.S., identify my clients' obstacles, and quickly move them through them so they can use the gifts they were given to live the life they have always dreamt about. I use my unique experience to help my clients' utilize specific proven techniques for reaching their goals. I connect, empathize, lovingly guide, and penetrate the mind in order to uncover the true self in lightning speed.

I am energized by the success of those I have helped. I love every interaction; we are all unique and whether I am helping you work through mind and body issues, confidence issues, financial stagnation, or finding your authentic self, you deserve the gift that I have to offer.

Transform Your Body ~ Transform You

Step into your power and ignite your life!

ABOUT THE AUTHOR

Kim Burger is a Master Coach changing lives through her life coaching business, Lightning Transformations. Through coaching, meal plans, and fitness routines, she helps her clients achieve health, wellness, and financial goals. You will look better, feel better, exude confidence, and have more energy utilizing Kim's techniques! For more information, please visit Kim's website at: www.LightningTransformations.com

www.Facebook.com/LightningTransformations

www.linkedin.com/in/LightningTransformations

www.youtube.com/user/FatFreeBurger

pinterest.com/FatFreeBurger

WHAT'S IN YOUR PORTFOLIO?

by Richard Hudson

What if I were to tell you that you own a secret portfolio of powerful investments? There's a good chance you don't know about it. From the time you were born, your parents started investing in your portfolio. Your friends, your teachers, and other influential people in your life have made contributions. Some contributions have even been made by strangers; people you'd be surprised to discover had access to your portfolio. And even though you may not have known of your portfolio's existence, you have made your own contributions over the years. Some were wise investments, others not so wise. Every day, minute, and second, the contents of your portfolio compound and continually grow in power and influence.

Whether you recognize it or not, this portfolio impacts and controls your life. When you run into obstacles or succeed beyond your wildest dreams, you may wonder why. Like most people, you may not understand the power of your portfolio. Some have discovered their portfolios, and through careful management have come to live

213

magnificent lives powered by their own investments. Others don't yet realize that they have a portfolio; however, they are intimately bound to the bad investments they have allowed to accumulate, which exert more and more control over their lives.

More than forty years ago I discovered my portfolio—a portfolio of beliefs. Beliefs are internal rules or programming that direct action. I realized that these beliefs could motivate and empower me or cripple and destroy me. My passion about beliefs comes from personal experience. I started out as a happy kid, but then something happened. In my twenties, I began suffering from bouts of severe depression. In many ways my life was good, but I was overwhelmed with sadness and anxiety. I found myself unable to function for weeks at a time. Fortunately, the other beliefs in my portfolio stopped me from seeking relief in drugs or alcohol. After a decade of despair, I discovered that just one belief was behind the depression. When I changed that one mistaken belief, my life changed, and I chose to radically transform my portfolio.

The good news is that whatever your beliefs, you can upgrade. Although you may not have been aware of what beliefs went into your portfolio, you do have control of what stays there. You can choose! Why not replace mediocre beliefs with a stunningly powerful, life-transforming investment: beliefs that work for you. This is what I show people how to do.

Maybe you're just starting to pay attention to what's in your portfolio of beliefs, and as you read about some of the areas I've explored, you might wonder what beliefs you'd like to upgrade.

Twenty-seven years ago I began an intense study of beliefs, the language that installs beliefs, and how beliefs operate in our lives. For more than two decades I worked as a corporate trainer and then as an executive coach. I showed CEOs and managing directors of multinational companies in fourteen countries on four continents how to develop powerful beliefs for business and personal success. Today I help all types of people discover and upgrade their own belief portfolios. Because most of our beliefs run on autopilot and are beneath the level of our awareness, it's sometimes difficult to recognize the beliefs that control us. They're so much a part of us that they may seem to be invisible. I help clients search for them with a Belief Assessment™ and then upgrade their portfolio with amazing, empowering beliefs.

I have a powerful belief that drives me: "There's got to be a way to do that and I ought to be able to find it." Not surprisingly, I love learning and teaching. My passion for understanding beliefs and the language patterns that create beliefs has led me to exciting research and applications beyond coaching. For example, I saw brilliant executives fall apart in front of an audience and wondered how that could be. My fascination with beliefs kicked in and, in 1990, I began a year-long study of confident public speakers. I studied their beliefs, behaviors, and strategies and found they share eight common elements. This groundbreaking study is the basis of *Speak Your Mind—Without Losing It*™, a two-day seminar at which I teach the beliefs of confident public speaking.

Then a few years ago, I recognized a pattern. Most of the issues my coaching clients faced, like my own battle with depression, were linked to beliefs they developed during childhood. I wondered if I could help kids develop powerful beliefs while they were still young. Because a primary role of parents is to teach their children beliefs, I interviewed a lot of moms and dads, most of whom had no idea how to pass their most valued beliefs on to their children. But it wasn't their fault—no one had taught them how. So now I teach parents how to build powerful, positive beliefs for themselves and how to pass them on to their children. One amazing way parents can do this is by proactively watching movies with their children. To show parents how to do this, I developed and produced a video series called, *The Movie-Savvy Parent—How to Use Cinematic Moments to Teach Character*.

Have you ever met someone who knew how to say just the right thing in a situation? As you found yourself fumbling for words, out of this person's mouth came a simple response that changed the entire situation and left you slack-jawed with admiration. Having a way with words can change beliefs and transform lives, and I want to spend my life doing that. When my coaching clients saw how I could help them shift beliefs, they wanted to learn my language strategies, so I developed *Language Power—How to Have a Way with Words*, for anyone who needs to communicate with influence.

What we say, the words and language patterns we use, often reveal the beliefs we hold. By listening to those patterns in others, we can see how their beliefs impact their results. I began to research and collect uncommon beliefs and language patterns that got amazing results. Some remarkable beliefs come from people you'd expect to have big, empowering beliefs like athletes, entrepreneurs, and influential leaders. Others come from people who hold an uncommon belief that leads them to extraordinary success in some areas of their lives.

How could symphony conductor James Levine's leadership beliefs change your business or family? What would it be like if you could take Mike Tyson's beliefs about training into your workday? What might you do with Joel Comm's beliefs for entrepreneurial and social media success? Those questions fascinate me, so I collect those beliefs in order to pass them on to others.

Now that you have begun to think about your portfolio of beliefs and where it can take you, consider what stunningly powerful, life-transforming beliefs you'd like to upgrade. The more you think about it, the more you'll want to explore your investment options, invest wisely, and enjoy your return on those investments. People say that changing beliefs is hard. But what if it's not? What if changing beliefs is as easy as changing out investments in your portfolio by just saying the word? Join me at BeliefBank.com to find out how.

ABOUT THE AUTHOR

Richard L. Hudson is the BeliefBanker™, the country's top expert on "The Most Important Investment You'll Ever Make™." An executive coach, speaker, and author, he has written a simple guide to giving a speech entitled, *70 Steps to Speaking Success.*

Hudson's book, *It's Time to Draw the Line—What Parents Must Do Now to Save Our Children and Restore Our National Treasure*, instructs parents on how to pass powerful beliefs and character to their children. His BeliefAbility™ Parenting podcasts are on ParentingBeliefs.com. Hudson also researches and spotlights remarkable, uncommon beliefs on his Belief Impact™ podcast and video blog at BeliefImpact.com.

facebook.com/richard.l.hudson1

twitter.com/richardlhudson

www.linkedin.com/pub/richard-l-hudson/7/4a8/863/

ABOUT THE AUTHOR

Joel Comm

Joel Comm is a New York Times Best-Selling author, Internationally-known speaker and Internet pioneer. Online since 1995, Joel has inspired, equipped and entertained millions of people through his web sites, software products, books, training and broadcasts. His previous titles include *The AdSense Code: What Google Never Told You About Making Money with AdSense, Click Here to Order: Stories of the World's Most Successful Internet Marketing Entrepreneurs, Twitter Power: How to Dominate Your Market One Tweet at a Time* and *KaChing: How to Run an Online Business that Pays and Pays.*